middot: a stairway of virtues

ron isaacs

ISBN #1-891662-71-6

Torah Aura Productions ▪ 4423 Fruitland Avenue, Los Angeles, CA 90058 (800) BE-Torah ▪ (800) 238-6724 ▪ (323) 585-7312 ▪ fax (323) 585-0327 E-MAIL <misrad@torahaura.com> ▪ Visit the Torah Aura website at www.torahaura.com

MANUFACTURED IN UNITED STATES OF AMERICA

contents

preface

The Hebrew word *middot*, from the Hebrew verb *madad* (to measure), has a number of related meanings. Rabbinic thinkers employed the term to describe people's types, temperaments, characteristics and dispositions. The term also refers to a collection of virtues that are intended to provide people with moral guidance for daily living. A virtuous person is called a *baal middot*, one who possesses good qualities. In *Ethics of the Fathers* two types of people are defined. "Whoever possesses generosity, humility and modesty is the disciple of our ancestor Abraham. Those who belong to the followers of wicked Balaam, however, possess an evil eye, a haughty spirit and excessive desire" *(Pirke Avot 5.22)*.

This sourcebook of Jewish virtues is intended to allow students to explore the practical wisdom that has informed Jewish piety throughout the centuries. This sourcebook includes a brief introduction to the genre of literature known as *musar*. This is followed by a presentation of twenty-five *middot*. Each moral virtue is accompanied by two entries from a traditional Jewish source. Follow-up questions allow the reader further opportunity to grapple with the meaning of the sources and other issues related to the *middah* under discussion.

I hope that this book will help students improve their understanding of ethical behavior and moral living. May these Jewish values guide them to live in a way that truly reflects God's image and to be the good and kind people that Judaism most values.

a brief history of the musar movement

There is no comprehensive concept in the Bible that parallels the modern concept of ethics. The first rabbinic listing of Jewish virtues is found in *Pirke Avot* 6.6. In *Pirke Avot* we are taught that the Torah is acquired through forty-eight virtues. The most notable virtues on the list are awe, fear, humility, patience, trust and generosity. During the medieval period the Hebrew term *musar* gradually acquired the connotation of moral principles and virtues that tend to improve the relationship between one person and another.

Yekhiel ben Yekutiel ben Binayamin ha-Rofe (late thirteenth century) was the author of an anthology entitled *Sefer Maalot ha-Middot* (*The Book of Choicest Virtues*). This anthology was the first in a new genre of literature, one that dealt with the analytic treatment of important Jewish virtues. Yekhiel taught each spiritual value and virtue by citing excerpts from the Bible and rabbinic literature. In order to define the virtues more graphically, he also categorized many vices that were antithetical to the virtues.

Written in the late twelfth century by Rabbi Yehuda Ha-Hasid, the ethical work *Sefer Hasidim* contains a rich variety of ethical and moral principles. The following is an example. "Call the attention of a non-Jew to an error he has made in overpaying you, for it is better that you live on charity than that you disgrace the Jewish name."

Rabbi Moses ben Nahman, called Ramban, represented the emotional, feeling side of Jewish ethics. In his famous *Iggeret Musar* (*Letter of Instruction*), which he wrote from the Holy Land shortly before he died in 1270, he told his son Nachman, "Learn to speak gently to all persons at all times. Regard every person as greater than yourself. When you address a person, do not keep staring in his face."

Rabbi Yehuda ibn Kalaaz, who lived in Algeria in the sixteenth century, wrote in his *Sefer ha-Musar*, "Reverence for God is the thread upon which the various good qualities of people are strung like pearls. When this string is severed, the pearls scatter in all directions and are lost one by one."

Orhot ha-Tzadikim (*The Ways of the Righteous*) is another book about virtues, published in Yiddish about five hundred years ago. Since the sixteenth century it has been printed in nearly eighty editions. Some of its major sections are devoted to pride, modesty, love, compassion, zeal, truth and repentance.

The fourteenth century ethical work *Menorat ha-Ma'or* is a summation of all phases of Jewish life. From this book a Jew learns the things he or she must do to be a true friend. "Be first to greet your fellow human being; invite him to your joyful occasions, call him by complimentary names; do not give away his secrets."

A movement known as the "*musar* movement" attempted to educate people about strict ethical behavior in the spirit of Jewish law. The movement was founded in the nineteenth century by Rabbi Israel Salanter, and he set up special houses for the study of Jewish ethics. He taught, "The sensual desire in man often makes him mistake momentary pleasure for the true happiness he craves, and he succumbs to the pressure of his passion. Frequent yielding to his sensual desires finally produces in man an impure spirit—the decay of his spiritual energy—with the result that he becomes a slave to his evil habits. We must train ourselves so that we no longer obey the ethical teachings reluctantly but follow them quite naturally."

Finally, Israel Meir Ha-Kohen, a nineteenth-century sage best known for his book *Hafetz Hayim* (*Desiring Life*), has been described as one of the moral geniuses of the Polish and Russian Jews. This saintly scholar discusses at length such misdemeanors as slander: "Those who listen to slanderous gossip are just as guilty as the talebearers. Repeated use of the evil tongue is like a silk thread made strong by hundreds of strands."

All of these teachers of ethics and virtues would likely agree that there is no rest for the good person, who must always strive to do better, to perfect the world and to increase righteousness. Such a person is likely to be humble, reliable, dependable, honest, unselfish, gracious, kind, compassionate and always sensitive to the feelings of others. The Yiddish word *mensch* aptly describes such a person—one who loves, respects and is devoted to his fellow human beings. A *mensch* will always look beyond the letter of the law to its spirit, living fully as a person who reflects God's truest image.

"My lowliness is my exaltedness." (Midrash, *Exodus Rabbah* 45.5)

1. humility—anavah

Moses, Judaism's greatest prophet, is described as being the humblest of men. "Moses was a very humble man, more than all the people that were upon the face of the earth" *(Numbers 12,3)*. Other famous Jews also valued humility. Abraham, considered the father of the Jewish people, says, "I have taken upon myself to speak to God, I who am but dust and ashes" *(Genesis 18.27)*. And the prophet Micah states, "God has told you what is good, and what God requires of you to do justice, love mercy and walk humbly with your God" *(Micah 6.8)*.

The ancient rabbis compare the Torah, God's greatest gift to people, to water. "Just as water flows downward, so the Torah that comes from on high flows only into the minds and hearts of the humble."

Rabbinic thinkers often warn people not to indulge in pride and arrogance. They assert that it is not enough to walk the moderate path of humility. Rather, they advise people to tend toward extreme modesty and even meekness in order to avoid being arrogant.

In Judaism meekness has been understood to mean gentleness to all people in both word and deed. It was wise King Solomon who once said, "And he that is of a low spirit shall attain honor" *(Proverbs 29.23)*.

From Our Tradition

the dispute of hillel and shammai

The following Talmudic tale deals with the historic rivalry between the followers of the sage Hillel and those of his contemporary Shammai. The school of Hillel usually interpreted the law in a liberal and lenient way, while the school of Shammai almost always held a strict, narrow line. Ultimately the school of Hillel triumphed, and its interpretations became the accepted standard of law.

> For three years the school of Shammai argued with the school of Hillel.
>
> The school of Shammai said, "The law agrees with our views."
>
> And the school of Hillel said, "The law agrees with our views."
>
> Then a Divine voice announced, "Both of these opinions are each the words of the living God.
>
> But the law follows the rulings of the school of Hillel."
>
> Why did the law follow the rulings of the school of Hillel if both schools' rulings are the words of the living God?
>
> Because the followers of Hillel were kind and modest.
>
> They not only studied the rulings of the school of Shammai, but even quoted these rulings before their own.
>
> This teaches that whoever acts humbly, the Holy Blessed One raises up, and whoever acts exalted, the Holy Blessed One humbles.
>
> From the person who seeks greatness, greatness flees. But the person who flees from greatness, greatness follows
>
> (Talmud, *Eruvin* 13b).

judge levi bar sissi

This tale, found in the *Genesis Rabbah*, concerns the unusual behavior of Judge Levi bar Sissi when the citizens of Simonia asked him to answer three questions.

When Rabbi Judah passed through the city of Simonia, the townspeople asked him to appoint a judge and teacher for them. He selected Levi bar Sissi. The people built a platform for bar Sissi to stand on when addressing them. But when they approached him with their questions, he found that he could no longer remember the answers. Troubled by this unusual problem, bar Sissi arose early in the morning and went to see Rabbi Judah. When Rabbi Judah saw bar Sissi, he asked, "What have the people of Simonia done?"

Levi bar Sissi answered, "They posed three questions to me, but I was unable to remember the answers. Then they repeated the questions, and I answered them correctly."

"If you know the answers," Rabbi Judah said, "then why did you not give them immediately upon being asked?"

Levi bar Sissi replied, "They put me on a platform and a tall chair. My spirit became conscious of the honor and the answers departed from me."

"Let this serve as an example to all," said Rabbi Judah. "When a person fills himself with pride, wisdom escapes him" *(Genesis Rabbah 81)*.

Questions

1. Have you ever had a competition with a classmate? Is it possible to stay humble during any competition? Do you agree with the statement in Talmud *Eruvin* 13, "From the person who seeks greatness, greatness flees. But the person who flees from greatness, greatness follows"? Can you cite an example of this statement?

2. *Genesis Rabbah* 81 says, "When people fill themselves with pride, wisdom escapes them." Can you think of an experience that bears out the truth of this statement? How do you think wisdom and pride are related?

3. According to the *Orhot Tzaddikim* (chapter 2), "The test of humility is one's attitude toward one's subordinates." What do you think is meant by this statement? What is your relationship to your subordinates?

4. Moses, considered by some the greatest prophet ever to have lived, raises a series of objections to God before he accepts his mission. Three of his objections follow. Read them, and decide whether his objections are in any way related to his humbleness. Can too much humility be counterproductive to good leadership?

   First Objection: After God has told Moses that he is the one who will be sent to Pharaoh to free the Israelites, Moses says, "Who am I that I should go to Pharaoh and free the Israelites from Egypt?" (Exodus 2.11)

   Second Objection: In Exodus 3.18 Moses is told by God, "The people will listen to you."

   Moses demurs and says, "What if they do not believe me, and do not listen to me?" (Exodus 4.1)

Third Objection: Moses says to God, "Please, God, I have never been a man of words. I am slow of speech and slow of tongue." (Exodus 4.10)

5. Throughout their day, Ḥasidim often use humility meditations to remind them of the importance of this trait. One such meditation is "Dust you are, and unto dust you shall return" (Genesis 3.19). If you were to choose a verse to use for a similar purpose, which one might it be?

6. Do you think that Moses was truly the humblest person on the face of the earth (Numbers 12.3)? Who gets your vote for the most humble person?

7. According to the Ḥasidic sage Rabbi Simḥa Bunim, all people should have two pockets so they can reach into one or the other, according to their needs. In the right pocket people should carry the words, "For my sake the world was created," and in the left, "I am earth and ashes." What would you advise putting into pockets?

8. According to the Talmud (*Bava Metzia* 23b), a scholar is permitted to declare that he is unfamiliar with a tractate of the Mishnah when asked a particular question. What do you think is the reason for this? How does it relate to our present topic?

2. repentance—t'shuvah

Great is repentance, because for the sake of the one
who truly repents, the whole world is pardoned.

(Talmud, *Yoma* 86b)

Most Jews are most likely to associate repentance with the
High Holy Days of Rosh ha-Shanah and Yom Kippur. The
ten day period from the start of the New Year until the end of
Yom Kippur is known as *aseret yemai t'shuvah*, the Ten Days of
Repentance. However, attendance at synagogue during these
days, even if accompanied by genuine repentance, only wins
forgiveness for offenses committed against God. As the Talmud
teaches, "The Day of Atonement atones for sins against God,
not for sins against man, unless the injured party has been ap-
peased" (Mishnah, *Yoma* 8.9).

In truth, the opportunity for *t'shuvah* (repentance) is not
restricted to any specific time. It is always available and is an
ongoing process. The Hebrew term for repentance, *t'shuvah*, literally means "to return," or "to change direction." In Judaism,
repentance is not enough to make up for a transgression. You
must do something of a diametrically opposed nature. You can't
just feel sorry and quit performing the bad deed. You must do
something to make up for it. Thus, Jewish repentance requires
a concerted effort on the part of the transgressor to break with
the past, do an about-face and perform better actions.

The great medieval philosopher Moses Maimonides devotes ten chapters to repentance in his work the *Mishnah Torah*.

Defining different grades of repentance, he offers this illustration.

> "If an opportunity presents itself for repeating an offense, and the offender, while *able* to commit the offense, nevertheless refrains from doing so because the offender is penitent but not out of fear or failure of energy, this is repentence. If, however, a person only repents in old age, at a time when that person is no longer capable of doing what s/he used to do, this is not an excellent mode of repentance; but it is acceptable."

According to Maimonides, even if one transgressed all one's life and only repented on the day of one's death, one's transgressions are pardoned.

> Rabbi Eliezer ben Hyrcanus said, "Repent one day before your death."

> His students asked him, "How is it possible for a person to repent one day before his death, since a person does not know when he shall die?"

> He replied, "All the more reason is there that a person should repent every day, lest he die the next day. Thus, all his days will be days of repentance"
>
> (Talmud, *Avot de Rabbi Natan* 15).

If you integrate repentance into your daily routine, *Pirke Avot* suggests that your entire life will become part of the process of personal change.

From Our Tradition

the story of the meat seller

This Talmudic tale attempts to illustrate the meaning of true repentance and to show how a person may be sure that another has repented.

> It was discovered that a certain meat vendor sold unfit meat. Rav Naḥman took away the man's license and disqualified him as a kosher slaughterer. As a sign of penitence, the man let his hair and beard grow and gave the appearance of doing repentance. Rav Naḥman was ready to restore his vendor's license to him, but Rabba said, "He may be a hypocrite. How shall we truly know when to grant him our confidence again?"
>
> Rabbi Iddi ben Abin suggested, "When he goes to a place where he is unknown and demonstrates that a mitzvah is more important to him than money, either by returning something which he has found or by condemning as unkosher valuable meat that belongs to him." (Talmud, *Sanhedrin* 25a)

eleazar ben dordia

This Talmudic tale attempts to teach us that true repentance must come from our heart and soul, and we cannot ask others to intercede on our behalf.

> It was told that Eleazar ben Dordia was a devotee of prostitutes. Once, when he heard that a certain prostitute lived near the sea, he took his purse filled with *dinars*, and he crossed seven rivers in order to reach her. When he was with her, she exhaled and said to him,

"Just as I have blown out the air that will never return, so you Eleazar ben Dordia will never be given forgiveness for your sins."

Eleazar went out and sat between two hills and said, "Hills, beg for kindness for me."

"How can we pray for you?" they answered. "We stand in need of compassion for ourselves, for it is written, 'For the mountains may move and the hills be shaken'" (*Isaiah* 54.10).

"Heaven and earth," he cried out, "you plead for kindness for me!"

"How can we pray for you?" they retorted. "We stand in need of compassion for ourselves, as it is said, 'The heavens shall melt away like smoke, and the earth wear out like clothing'" (*Isaiah* 51.16).

"Sun and moon," he shouted, "you plead for me!"

"How can we intercede for you?" they answered. "We stand in need of compassion for ourselves, as it is said, 'Then the moon shall be ashamed and the sun shall be humiliated'" (*Isaiah* 24.23).

"Stars and planets," Eleazar called out, "you plead for me."

"How can we?" they answered. "We also need mercy for ourselves, as it is written, 'All the heavenly hosts shall molder'" (*Isaiah* 34.4).

"Then," he said, "This matter solely depends on me." He put his head between his knees and cried aloud until his soul left him.

Just then a *bat kol* (heavenly voice) was heard saying, "Rabbi Eleazar ben Dordia is destined for the world to come."

When Rabbi Judah the Prince heard this, he cried and said, "There are those who attain the world to come after many years, and some in just one hour!" He also said, "Penitents are not only accepted, they are even called 'Rabbi'" (Talmud, *Avodah Zarah* 17a).

Questions

1. In the story of the meat vendor in Talmud *Sanhedrin* 25a, the question is how to know whether one who seems to have repented has truly done so. What is your litmus test for determining true repentance?

2. What is the moral of the Eleazar ben Dordia story? What do we learn from it about the meaning of true repentance?

3. According to Rav Naḥman of Bratslav, there are three requisites for repentance: seeing eyes, hearing ears, and an understanding heart that is ready to return and be healed. Let your eyes see your conduct, let your ears hear words of criticism and let your heart understand its eternal purpose. Then you will attain perfect repentance. What are your standards for repentance? Is there, in your opinion, such a thing as "perfect repentance"?

4. According to *Sefer Ḥasidim*, the most admirable kind of repentance takes place when a strong, vigorous person subdues an overwhelming urge, rather than when a person incapable of action fails to act on an urge. What is your opinion of this *Sefer Ḥasidim* text? In your opinion, what is the most admirable kind of repentance?

5. In his *Gates of Repentance,* Jonah Gerondi wrote that the repentant sinner should strive to do good deeds with the same faculties or parts of the body with which he or she sinned. Thus, if one's feet ran to sin, they should now run to perform good deeds. If one's mouth spoke falsehoods, it should now speak wisdom. Hands that were violent should now open in charity. What are your thoughts about Gerondi's advice? Which parts of the body are most likely to get a person into trouble?

6. *Pirke Avot* 2.1 states that when a person thinks about three things, he or she will be able to overcome the desire to sin. "Know what is above, a seeing eye, an ear that hears and a book in which all your actions are recorded." In the space provided, write your own modern version of things that will help overcome one's desire to sin.

   Modern Version. A person can overcome the desire to sin when _____

7. Rabbi Meir said that when one truly repents, the entire world is pardoned (Talmud, *Yoma* 86b). What do you think Rabbi Meir meant by this statement?

8. In the last few years people have been faxing requests for God's intervention to the Western Wall. People in the Hasidic world are also asking for forgiveness by e-mail. The e-mails and faxes are placed on the grave of the Lubavitcher Rebbe, Menachem Mendel Schneerson. How do you feel about people sending e-mails and faxes to ask for forgiveness? How do you feel about the use of the telephone to ask for forgiveness?

9. The Talmud *Yoma* 86b asks, "How can one prove that one is truly penitent? Rabbi Judah said, 'If an opportunity to commit the same sin presents itself on two occasions and

one does not yield to it.'" How would you answer the same question?

10. According to Rabbi Moshe Teitelbaum, you should turn your mind to repentance before you pray, before studying Torah and before eating. What do you think are the best times to turn your mind toward repentance?

11. Rabbi Elijah deVidas advised people to make some sort of alteration to their food and drink and to their clothing in order to remember to do *t'shuvah* each and every day. For example, he suggested that one week a person ought not eat fruit, another week not eat hot food, and so on. What are your thoughts about this suggestion? How would you advise a person to remember to do daily *t'shuvah*?

Friendship—Yedidut

3. friendship——yedidut

"Get yourself a companion" (*Pirke Avot* 1.6).

"...Get yourself a companion," advised Joshua ben Perakhya. People often have many acquaintances, but there are few people who have more than one or two good friends.

Jonathan and David's model friendship in the Bible (in the first book of Samuel) is held in high esteem. What makes their friendship especially remarkable is that these two men had competitive interests. Jonathan was the oldest son of King Saul and heir apparent to the throne. David, King Saul's leading soldier, was the people's choice to be the future king. Yet their potential competition never stood in the way of their friendship. David's gift of leadership only increased Jonathan's desire to be the top aide in his friend's future kingdom. "You are going to be king over Israel and I shall be second to you" (*I Samuel* 23.17).

You are no doubt beginning to feel the pressures. Having a close friend or two can go a long way to alleviate some of the stresses and frustrations. Since friendships such David and Jonathan's are rather unusual, Judaism urges you to be very careful when choosing your friends.

From Our Tradition

three friends

This tale, adapted from *Pirke de Rabbi Eleazar,* an eighth-century midrashic work, tells the story of an extremely agitated person who needs friendship for comfort and the extent to which each of his friends would help him.

A man had three friends. One friend he loved very much, the second he loved as well. The third friend was regarded with less affection. Once the king commanded this man to appear before him. He was extremely agitated, wondering what the king might have in mind. With fear and trepidation the person called upon each of his three friends to accompany him to his meeting with the king.

First he turned to his most beloved friend and was extremely disappointed that this friend was unable to attend his meeting with the king.

When he turned to his second friend, the friend replied that he would go with him, but only so far as the gates of the palace and no further.

Finally, and with a touch of desperation, he turned to the friend to whom he had been the least devoted. The third friend said, "I will not only go with you before the king, but I will plead your case as well."

Who is the first friend? It is wealth and material things that one must leave behind when one departs this world, as it is written, "Riches profit not in the day of reckoning" (Proverbs 11.4).

Who is the second friend? It is one's relatives, who can only follow one to the graveside, as it is written, "No person can by any means redeem a fellow person from death" (Psalms 49.8).

The third friend, the least considered one, is made up of the good deeds of a person's life. These never leave one, and they even precede one to plead one's cause before the King of Kings, as it is written, "And your righteousness shall go before you" (Psalm 85.13). (*Pirke de Rabbi Eleazar*)

Questions

1. Do you have friends who can be compared to the kinds of friends discussed in the above story?

2. Do you agree with the comparisons made in the story?

3. What is the moral of the story? Do you agree with that moral?

4. Think of the very first person with whom you wanted to be friends. Why did you choose him or her? Is he or she still your friend today?

5. Suppose that you and your close friend are neck and neck in the race to be valedictorian of your senior class. Do you think you could both pursue this goal and still remain good friends?

6. *Menorat ha-Maor*, a biblical commentary, gives advice to a person who wants to show that he or she is truly a friend.

    Be first to greet your friend, invite your friend to your joyful occasions, call your friend by complimentary names, never give away your friend's secrets, help when your friend is in trouble, look after your friend's interests when your friend is away, overlook your friend's shortcomings and forgive your friend promptly, criticize when your friend has done wrong, respect your friend always, do not deceive your friend, do not lie to your friend, pray for your friend and wish your friend happiness, arrange a burial if your friend dies.

What advice would you give to someone who wants to show that he or she is truly worthy of being a friend?

List your advice for friendship.

1. _____

2. _____

3. _____

4. _____

5. _____

the separated friends

This legend about two friends demonstrates the commitment that one friend has for the other, even when life itself is on the line. The story is also an illustration of the advice in *Ethics of the Fathers*, "Get yourself a companion" *(Pirke Avot 1.6)*.

There were two close friends who had been separated by war so that they lived in different kingdoms. Once one of them went to visit his friend, and because he came from the city of the king's enemy, he was imprisoned and sentenced to be executed as a spy.

No amount of pleading would save him, so he begged the king for kindness.

"Your majesty," he said, "let me have just one month to return to my land and put my affairs in order so my family will be cared for after my death. At the end of the month I will return to pay the penalty."

"How can I believe you will return?" asked the king. "What security can you offer?"

"My friend will be my security," said the man. "He will pay for my life with his if I do not return."

The king called in the man's friend, and to his amazement, the friend agreed to the conditions.

On the last day of the month the sun was setting, and the man had not yet returned. The king ordered the man's friend killed in his stead. As the sword was about to descend the man returned and quickly placed the sword on his own neck. But his friend stopped him. "Let me die for you," he pleaded.

The king was deeply moved. He ordered the sword taken away and pardoned both of them.

"Since there is such great love and friendship between the two of you," he said, "I entreat you to let me join you as a third."

And from that day on the two friends became the king's companions. And it was in this spirit that our sages of blessed memory said, "Get yourself a companion."

(*Beit ha-Midrash*, Adolf Jellinek)

Questions

1. Do you think that the friends' commitment to each other in this story goes beyond reason? Can you think of a modern-day example of someone who went to great trouble for a friend?

2. How can two friends gain additional friends together? Does this story provide any advice?

3. What must one do to keep a friendship strong? Why do you think that some friendships dissolve quickly, while others last much longer? What makes for a long-lasting friendship?

4. How much should you inconvenience yourself for a friend? Would you speak up for your friend even though it might hurt you?

5. We are told in *Avot de Rabbi Natan* 23 that a true leader is one who can turn an enemy into a friend. Can you think of an example of someone who was able to do this?

6. Recent studies have shown that the following traits are highly desirable in attracting friends. With a partner in your class, share your feelings about each of these traits. Then talk to your partner about other character traits of people with whom you are most likely to become friends.

   Pleasantness

   Considerateness

   Reliability

   Sense of humor

   Standing up for one's convictions

   Ability to carry on a conversation

4. common decency— derekh eretz

The answer "yes" (to a knock on the door) does not mean "enter" but "wait" (Talmud, *Bava Kamma* 33a).

The Hebrew term *derekh eretz* (literally, "the way of the land") is difficult to define exactly. It has often been used to connote decency, decorum, proper etiquette, good manners, common courtesy and even savoir faire. The term definitely has ethical implications, for as a whole it refers to a code of proper behavior toward people.

Rabbinic literature is filled with rules and suggestions on dignified conduct, common courtesy and good manners. It covers almost every aspect of a person's behavior, including seemingly insignificant things. Areas covered include how to speak, how to dress, how to walk, how to eat and drink, how to treat other people and how to conduct one's personal relationships.

From Our Tradition
how to love

This tale, told by Rabbi Moshe Leib Sassover, teaches an important lesson about how one ought to treat a fellow human being.

Rabbi Moshe Leib Sassover used to say, "I learned from a peasant how to love my fellow Jews. Once at a party I heard a drunken peasant say to his friend, 'Do you love me or not?'

The other answered, 'I love you greatly.'

The first peasant asked, 'Do you know what I need?'

'How can I possibly know what you need?' came the reply.

'How then,' said the peasant, 'can you say that you love me, when you don't know what I need?'"

From this Reb Moshe Leib learned to love Israel. "Feel their needs, know their pain, be part of their suffering."

Questions

1. According to this story, what are the most important abilities for one person to show love to another? Do you agree that love includes these abilities?

2. According to the Talmud (*Rosh ha-Shanah* 16b), a student should visit his teacher every holiday. According to the Talmud (*Derekh Eretz Rabbah,* chapter 5), a person should never leave the company of his teacher, or even his fellow students, unless first obtaining permission to do so. What common courtesies do you believe a student ought to afford a teacher? What common courtesies do you believe students ought to extend to their classes?

3. Rabbi Eleazar ben Azariah (*Pirke Avot* 3.23) said, "If there is no Torah, there is no *derekh eretz*, and if there is no *derekh eretz*,

there is no Torah." What do you think he meant by this statement?

4. How often do you compliment other people? Do you feel that you receive enough compliments in your daily life, or would you like to receive more of them?

how to compliment a bride

This Talmudic text presents the views of both Rabbi Hillel and Rabbi Shammai as they attempt to answer the question of how one should compliment a bride even if one feels that she is not particularly good-looking. Rabbi Hillel was known to be less stringent and rigorous than Rabbi Shammai, and more often than not his views have been accepted as custom.

Our rabbis asked, "How does one compliment a bride?"

Bet Shammai says, "A bride as she is."

But Bet Hillel says, "A beautiful and graceful bride."

Bet Shammai said to Bet Hillel, "If she were lame or blind, would you still call her 'a beautiful and graceful bride,' since the Torah says, 'Keep far from falsehood'" *(Exodus 23.7)*?

Bet Hillel said to Bet Shammai, "According to you, when someone makes a bad purchase in the market should you praise it before him, or defame it? Surely you should praise it. Therefore, the sages concluded, 'One should always be pleasant toward people'"

(Talmud, *Ketubot* 16b-17a).

33

Questions

1. In the case of a bride, do you agree with Bet Hillel that one should "fudge" the truth in order to make her feel good? Are there other times when common decency warrants fudging the truth to protect another's feelings? Would you compliment a person regardless of whether or not that person deserved the compliment?

2. Have you ever had a teacher you called by his or her first name? Why did you do so? Is it disrespectful, as the rabbis have often stated, to call a teacher by a first name?

3. According to the Talmud (*Derekh Eretz Zutah,* chapter 6), one should not sit down at a table to eat before one's elders have taken their seats. What are some other nice things that one can do for one's elders?

4. "Running up the score" in sports means trying to score as many points as possible, even when you are already far ahead in the game. Some people believe that running up the score is bad sportsmanship and lacks respect for one's opponent. Others feel that you play sports to win the game, and it is insulting to the losing team if the winning team stops trying. What do you think? Is it proper *derekh eretz* to run up the score in a game that is clearly a mismatch?

5. Can one be a decent person and be ignorant of Torah? Why do you think Judaism commands us to act with common decency?

5. keeping commitments— hithayevut

It is better to make no promises at all than to make them, even if one is certain of fulfilling them.

(Talmud, *Hullin* 2a)

Whether one calls it a vow, a promise or simply one's word, all Jewish views emphasize the importance of keeping a commitment. One's word is tied to one's belief in God and in God's presence in the world and our lives. The Torah teaches (*Numbers* 30.3) that a person who makes a vow, who makes a promise to God or who takes an oath to do something must carry out that promise. The third of the Ten Commandments obligates a person not to utter the name of God in a promise in vain.

The most comprehensive of all Jewish law codes, the *Shulhan Arukh*, devotes many chapters to the laws of promises and vows. As an example of how seriously the Jewish community considered vows, the opening chapter on vows in the *Code of Jewish Law* states, "Do not be in the habit of making vows. The one who does make a vow is called wicked."

From Our Tradition

the falsely accused jew

This story from *Sefer Hasidim* describes the dilemma of a Jew who was put on trial and required to take an oath, even though he was in the habit of not doing so.

It once happened that gentiles falsely accused a Jew of a crime. The Jew was put on trial and was required to take an oath. He swore truthfully, declaring himself innocent of the charges. Afterwards he said to the rabbi, "Although I told the truth, I regret taking the oath and uttering God's name. My father and mother never took an oath, even a true one, as long as they were alive. I was compelled to swear, and I did so against my will, since otherwise I would have been condemned to death."

The rabbi answered, "If you want to atone for this, you should resolve never again to utter God's name, either to affirm a true statement or in vain, in German or in any other language, as people are in the habit of saying, 'May God help us.' Do not use such expressions. Enunciate God's name only when you are reading biblical verses or pray. Do not do business with a person unless you can trust him without having to resort to taking an oath, so that you will not be drawn into a situation where you will have to swear."

Questions

1. How often do you find yourself making a vow or a promise? Did you ever make a promise that you were unable to keep? Are there times when we can make promises we have no intention of keeping?

2. Why do you think that Jewish tradition urges people not to make promises or vows?

3. According to *Ethics of the Fathers* 3.13, "Vows are meant to be a fence for abstinence." What do you think this means?

4. The *Zohar*, the *Book of Mysticism,* asks, "What is a desirable oath?" It answers, "If an evil impulse is leading you away from the performance of a commandment, take an oath that you will perform the commandment." How would you answer the question, "What is a desirable oath?"

the vows of the kol nidre prayer

One of the best-known statements about promises and vows comes from the Day of Atonement, Yom Kippur, in the form of the Kol Nidre prayer. This unusual declaration specifies that all our unfulfilled promises to God are null and void. It has been said that Kol Nidre was originally designed to protect Jews who had been forced to convert to Christianity in order to save their lives. It allowed them to make Christian promises without being afraid that they had turned their backs on Judaism.

> All vows, promises, obligations and oaths to God where-with we have vowed, sworn and bound ourselves from this Day of Atonement till the next day of Atonement, may it come to us for good. Of all these, we repent us in them. They shall be absolved, released, annulled, made void and of no effect. They shall not be binding, nor shall they have any power. Our vows to God shall not be vows, and our bonds shall not be bonds, and our oaths shall not be oaths. (Kol Nidre prayer)

Questions

1. Were there any vows you made to God this year that you want to be annulled? There is a custom to have the cantor recite the Kol Nidre prayer three times in succession. Why do you think this is?

2. Rabbi Eliezer once said (Talmud, *Shevuot* 36a) "Yes is an oath, and no is an oath." What do you think he meant by this? Can you give an example?

3. What do you think should happen to people who do not keep their promises?

4. Are there any times when it is important to make promises?

6. lovingkindness—
gemilut hasadim

> The world rests on three things—on Torah, on service
> to God and on deeds of lovingkindness (Pirke Avot 1.2).

The practice of *gemilut hasadim*, deeds of kindness, includes every kind of help: visiting the sick, comforting the mourners, escorting the dead to the grave. The Mishnah (*Peah* 1.2) counts it among the things for which no limit has been prescribed by the Torah. Since *gemilut hasadim* consists of personal acts of kindness, it can be practiced by rich and poor alike.

Hesed, kindness, is one of the terms the Torah uses in describing God's attributes (*Numbers* 14.18). We become more like God when we act lovingly and with kindness, when we perform *gemilut hasadim*, because we are acknowledging that we have an effect on the world.

From Our Tradition
the gates of righteousness

This tale attempts to explain what King David meant when he said, "Open to me the gates of righteousness" and the way in which a soul is allowed to gain entrance into the world to come.

King David said, "Open to me the gates of righteousness" (Psalm 118.19). Why did King David ask that the gates be opened to him, rather than the gate?

In the world to come souls are asked, "What good did you perform on behalf of your fellow human beings?"

If a soul says in truth, "I have fed the hungry," the response is, "This is a gate unto God. Those who have fed the hungry may enter into it."

If a soul says, "I gave drink to the thirsty, I clothed the naked, I brought up an orphan, I gave charity, I labored in mercy," the response is, "This is a gate unto God. Those who gave drink to the thirsty may enter into it." The same is true with respect to other deeds.

But King David said, "I did all of these things. Therefore, open to me all the gates" (Shocher Tov 118).

Questions

1. According to the above text, what kind of behavior will ensure one's place in the world to come?

2. Rabbi Eleazar said, "Loving acts of kindness are greater than charity, for it is said, 'Sow for yourselves according to charity, but reap according to your lovingkindness.'" (Hosea 10.12) What do you think is meant by this statement?

3. The philosopher Maimonides said that if a poor person who is unknown to you says, "I am hungry, give me something to eat," you should not suspect a deception and respond with questions aimed at uncovering it. Instead, you should feed the poor person at once (Mishnah Torah, "Laws of Gifts to the Poor," 7.6). Do you agree with Maimonides? What if the beggar is a phony?

i desire love and not sacrifice (avot de rabbi natan, a4)

This teaching attempts to explain the statement from *Hosea*, "I desire love and not sacrifice."

> Simon the Just said, "Upon three things the world is based: upon Torah, upon the Temple service, and upon the performance of *gemilut hasadim*." With regard to the third, it is said, "I desire love and not sacrifice" (*Hosea* 6.6). The world at the beginning was created only by love, as it is said, "The world is built by love" (Psalms 89.3).
>
> It happened that Rabbi Yohanan ben Zakkai went out from Jerusalem, and Rabbi Joshua followed him. Rabbi Joshua saw the ruins of the Temple and said, "Woe is it that the place where the sins of Israel find atonement is laid waste."
>
> Then said Rabbi Yohanan, "Grieve not. We have an atonement equal to the Temple: the performance of *gemilut hasadim*, as it is said, 'I desire love and not sacrifice'" (*Avot de Rabbi Natan* 11a).

Questions

1. What does the statement "I desire love and not sacrifice" mean? In what way are deeds of *gemilut hasadim* an atonement?

2. According to Rabbi Simlai (Talmud, *Sotah* 14a), "The Torah begins with deeds of lovingkindness and ends with deeds of lovingkindness." Look up the verses in Genesis 3.21 and Deuteronomy 34.6 to see illustrations of Rabbi Simlai's statement.

3. Which is more difficult, giving money to charity (*tzedakah*) or doing a deed of lovingkindness?

4. Rabbi Yohanan once said, "Be always like a helmsman, on the lookout for good deeds" (*Leviticus Rabbah* 21.5). What do you think he meant by this statement?

7. hospitality— hakhnasat orhim

Let your house be open wide. Treat the poor as members of your own family. *(Pirke Avot 1.4)*

In contemporary circles hospitality is generally regarded as no more than etiquette. However, in Jewish tradition hospitality to guests and strangers has been elevated to one of the essential religious obligations.

Throughout the history of the Jewish people hospitality to guests has been a standard of proper Jewish manners. This mitzvah has developed into a means of showing personal and community concern for travelers and other guests. Welcoming strangers warmly and helping to satisfy their need for food, lodging and participation in religious celebrations grew to mean including friends and relatives, as well as travelers, in the joy of Sabbath and festival meals. Hosting a guest for the Sabbath or a festival became a sign of status in Jewish communities around the world.

From Our Tradition
abraham's visitors

In this biblical story Abraham has just been circumcised and must be in pain. Nevertheless, he hastens to welcome his unannounced guests, providing them with food and drink.

And God appeared to Abraham by the terebinths of Mamre. Abraham was sitting at the entrance of the tent as the day grew very hot. Looking up, he saw three men standing near him. As soon as he saw them, he ran from the entrance of the tent to greet them, and bowing to the ground, he said, "My lords, if it please you, do not go on past your servant. Let a little water be brought, and bathe your feet and recline under this tree. And let me get you a morsel of bread that you may refresh yourselves. Then go on, seeing that you have come your servant's way."

They replied, "Do as you have said."

Abraham hastened into the tent of Sarah and said, "Hurry, get three measures of choice flour. Knead and make cakes." Then Abraham ran to the herd, took a calf, tender and choice, and gave it to a servant boy, who hastened to prepare it. Abraham took curds and milk and the calf that had been prepared, and he set these before his guests. And he waited on them under the tree as they ate (*Genesis* 18.1-8).

Questions

1. Based on the story above, Abraham became known as a man of hospitality. What do you think makes Abraham's actions in this story so exemplary?

2. How do you feel about showing hospitality to strangers? What actions would indicate that you welcome people with whom you are not yet acquainted?

3. Should strangers and guests respond in any special way when you extend gestures of friendship and hospitality?

How do you expect your guests to behave in order to show appreciation for your thoughtfulness?

one dish short

This midrashic story tells of a banquet for Roman nobles in which the host fails to prepare enough dishes for each of his guests.

Once Bar Yohania decided to give a banquet for the nobles of Rome. He consulted with Rabbi Eliezer ben Yosi Ha-Gelili. Rabbi Eliezer said, "If you intend to invite twenty, prepare enough for twenty-five, and if you intend to invite twenty-five, prepare enough for thirty." However, Bar Yohania prepared only enough for twenty-four and then invited twenty-five. He brought a gold dish and placed it before the guest who had no food. The guest tossed it in his face, saying, "Do I eat gold?"

Bar Yohania went to Rabbi Eliezer ben Yose and said to him, "I ought not to tell you this, for you told me what to do and I did not do it. But I want to know, has God revealed to you scholars the secrets of the Torah and the secrets of entertaining as well?"

Rabbi Eliezer answered, "God has revealed to us the secrets of entertaining as well."

"How did you know what to do?" Bar Yohania asked.

Rabbi Eliezer answered, "From David, because it is written, 'When Abner came to David in Hebron, accompanied by twelve men, David made a feast for Abner and the men with him' (*II Samuel* 3.20). It does not simply say, 'He made a feast,' but it also says 'for the men with him'" *(Esther Rabbah,* chapter 2, section 4).

Questions

1. What is the moral of the story of Bar Yoḥania's banquet?

2. What do you do to make your guests feel welcome and comfortable?

3. What kind of guests do you most enjoy having at your house? Why?

4. Who do you feel benefits more from hospitality, the guest or the host? Who do you feel ought to benefit the most? Does hospitality have to benefit anyone?

8. leadership——hanhagah

Who is the leader of all leaders? One who can make
an enemy into a friend. (*Avot de Rabbi Natan 23*)

One way of learning about a society's values is by analyzing its leaders. A leader should embody all the values that his or her group holds dear. Judaism has always lauded good leadership. A true leader in Judaism is generally understood to be one who shows the way, guiding and directing by virtue of wisdom, experience or the confidence we place in him or her. A good leader uses the resources of a group, particularly the human resources, to achieve a goal that the members of the group hold important.

The biblical King David is an example of a well-respected Jewish leader. His lifetime of accomplishments is documented in the Books of Samuel and the First Book of Kings.

From Our Tradition

david and the goats

The following midrash suggests that it was King David's early life as a herdsman that helped prepare him for a position of leadership.

David would bring the young goats to feed on the tender tops of the grasses, the older goats he would bring to feed on the mature grasses, which were of medium consistency, and he would bring the fully mature goats to feed on the tough roots of the grasses. The Holy One said, "One who knows so well how to herd the flock each according to its strength shall come to herd my flock the people of Israel" (*Yalkut Shimoni*, Psalm 78).

Questions

1. What does the midrash about David and the goats teach us about his ability to be a leader? What are the qualities of leadership depicted in this midrash?

2. Maimonides, the great medieval philosopher, identified a system of priorities in the Torah, in which it was understood that the people needed effective and committed leadership before they could make their home in the land of Israel and establish the Temple. The king, the ancient leader in biblical times, had to meet four minimal standards before he could be appointed.

   a. One must be a born Jew.

   b. One must be pious.

   c. One must ascend to the throne to fulfill a mitzvah.

   d. One must be willing to fulfill the specific mitzvot of a king.

   What are your criteria for good leadership?

3. The Talmud (*Avot de Rabbi Natan* 23) says that a leader is one who makes an enemy into a friend. Do you think it is possible to turn an enemy into a friend?

4. Name some people you believe are good leaders (past and present).

joseph, the hated brother of reuven and judah

Jacob was the third of the Jewish patriarchs. He had twelve sons and one daughter with four different women who were his wives or concubines. His favorite wife was Rachel, and her eldest son was Joseph. Jacob favored Joseph above all of his other children, and he gave him a multi-colored cloak. Resentment quickly grew among the brothers, and one day when Joseph came out to the fields in which they worked they plotted to kill him.

> And the brothers said to one another, "Look, this dreamer is coming. Now let us kill him and throw him into one of the pits, and we will say, 'An evil beast has eaten him.' We will see what becomes of his dreams."
>
> And Reuven heard them and rescued Joseph from them, saying, "Let us not take his life." And Reuven said to them, "Shed no blood. Throw him into this pit in the wilderness, but do not lay a hand on him." He meant to rescue Joseph from his brothers' hands and return him to his father. So when Joseph came to his brothers, they stripped him of his coat of many colors that he was wearing, and they took him and threw him into the pit, an empty pit with no water. They sat down to eat bread, and they looked up and saw a band of Ishmaelites coming from Gil'ad with their camels bearing spices, balm and jewels, on their way down to Egypt. And Judah said to his brothers, "What is the profit in killing our brother and hiding his blood? Come, let us sell him to the Ishmaelites, and let our hand not be upon him, for he is our brother, our flesh." And his brothers listened to him (*Genesis* 37.19-27).

Questions

1. Who in your estimation, Judah or Reuven, displayed the stronger leadership? The rabbis reviewed this story in terms of Reuven and Judah's actions, and they made some interesting comments. Read their comments, and then decide who the rabbis felt was the better leader.

    a. Judah's protest is evidence that the Israelites observed the Ten Commandments even before the Torah was given, because Judah knew that we were not to commit murder.

    b. Reuven persuaded his brothers not to commit murder, but Judah convinced them that they would be just as guilty of murder by neglect as they would be of murder by action.

    c. Judah's actions did not go far enough. Because the Bible states, "and his brothers listened to him," the sages held that the brothers would have listened had Judah said to rescue Joseph (i.e., Judah started the process of redemption but did not complete it).

2. Can you think of examples within your group of times when two members tried to lead in different directions? What were the results? Were the discussions (or perhaps arguments) focused on the different directions, or were there issues of leadership at the core?

3. If you could be a leader of any organization (current or past), what would it be, and why would you want to lead it?

4. Ben Zoma once taught, "Who is a leader? One who controls one's passions and emotions" (*Pirke Avot* 4.1). How would you answer the question "Who is a leader?"

5. Rabbi Nahman of Bretslav once said that when a person is able to take abuse with a smile, that person is worthy to become a leader. Do you know such a person? Is it ever possible to take abuse with a smile?

9. charity—tzedakah

The person who gives to the poor shall not lack.

(Proverbs 28.27)

Although the Hebrew word *tzedakah* is often understood and translated as "charity," this translation does not convey all that tzedakah implies. The word is derived from the biblical word *tzedek*, meaning "righteousness" or "justice." Thus, in Jewish thinking, tzedakah is not only a matter of philanthropic sentiment, but an act of justice. Jews are obligated to give not because helping others is a kind thing to do, but because righteous giving helps to eliminate injustice in the world.

From Our Tradition

rabbi akiba's daughter

Charity was known to have a redemptive aspect to it. Following is an interesting tale about the advice an astrologer gave to Rabbi Akiba, whose daughter was to be married.

An astrologer told Rabbi Akiba that on the day his daughter was to enter the bridal chamber a snake would bite her and she would die.

As the wedding approached Rabbi Akiba became more and more worried. On the day of her marriage the bride took a brooch and stuck it into the wall, where, by chance, the pin penetrated the eye of a poisonous snake. The next morning, when she pulled the brooch from the wall, the dead snake dropped to the ground. Overjoyed that she had survived the fateful night, Rabbi Akiba asked her, "What did you do to be saved?"

She replied, "A poor man came to our door in the evening while everyone was busy at the banquet. Since there was no one to attend to him, I took the portion that was given to me and gave it to him."

"You have done a good deed," Rabbi Akiba said to her.

Thereupon he went out and taught, "Charity delivers from death itself" (Talmud, *Shabbat*, 156b).

Questions

1. What is the moral of the story of Rabbi Akiba? In what way does "charity deliver from death"?

2. What words describe the way you feel when you give tzedakah? To which organizations do you most enjoy giving?

3. The rabbis once said that a person who gives tzedakah without anyone knowing about it is greater than Moses. Do you think that a person who gives tzedakah anonymously is more commendable than one who wants everyone to know about his or her tzedakah gift?

the generous abba yudan

This midrashic story tells the story of the good-hearted Abba Yudan, a man who lost his fortune. His name was later changed to Abba Yudan the Cheater. This story explains why his name was changed.

As they went out to collect money for the school, Rabbi Eliezer, Rabbi Joshua and Rabbi Akiba encountered a good-hearted man, Abba Yudan, on the outskirts of Antioch. He had lost his entire fortune, and he only had one half of his field left. He asked his wife's advice, and she answered, "Sell half the field, and give your usual donation."

The rabbis blessed him, saying, "May God restore your prosperity."

Abba Yudan went forth to plow the remaining half of the field, and his ox stumbled on a stone and became lame. Beneath the stone Abba Yudan discovered a small chest filled with coins of the realm. He prospered greatly, and when the rabbis again came on their annual visit people said, "Abba Yudan is a man of many servants, cattle and camels. Who can expect to merit the sight of this wealthy man's countenance?"

When Abba Yudan met the rabbis, he said, "Your blessing has brought me fruit and the fruit of fruits."

They replied, "Though others have given more, your name has always headed the list of donors."

When he collected in Botzrah, Rabbi Simeon ben Lakish heard the name of the wealthy man as Abba Yudan the Cheater. He was told that this man would add up the donations of every Jew in the city and give as much as all of them together. This prompted people to give more than they usually would, and therefore Abba Yudan cheated them out of money (*Leviticus Rabbah* 5).

Questions

1. What is the moral of the Abba Yudan story? Do you know any people who are known for their very generous giving? Does generous gift giving encourage people to increase their gifts?

2. Many synagogues publish a list of the people who give to a particular campaign. Sometimes they also publish the monetary amounts of the donors' gifts. Do you think that this is a good idea? Why or why not?

3. *Pirke Avot* 5.16 describes four different kinds of people who give tzedakah: "The person who wants to give but believes that others should not give; the person who wants others to give but will not give himself; the person who gives and wants others to give; and finally, the person who will not give and does not want others to give." What do you think motivates each of these types of people? Do you know people who fit into these categories? What can you do to change their attitude about giving?

4. If you were given $100,000 and told to use it for tzedakah, how would you apportion the money? What guidelines might you suggest for deciding to whom money ought to be given?

10. peace——shalom

The world rests on three things: Justice, truth and peace.

(Pirke Avot 1.18)

The word *shalom*, used as a greeting or a farewell, can be best translated as completeness or wholeness. Although often translated as peace, it signifies welfare of every kind: contentment, security, prosperity, friendship and tranquility of mind and heart. When Jewish tradition speaks of shalom, it does not mean merely an absence of strife. Shalom implies a striving for harmony and unity among people despite their differences. A peace-pursuing person is held in the highest esteem in Judaism. In fact, the person who loves and pursues peace is regarded as a disciple of Aaron, the High Priest.

Shalom is also a name for God. This implies that peace is an integral element of God's essence and nature and a foundation for the very existence of the world and its people.

The *Book of Psalms* 34.14 says, "Seek peace, and pursue it." The Torah does not obligate us to pursue the mitzvot, only to fulfill them at the proper times. However, we are obliged to seek peace and pursue it at all times, both at home and away from home.

From Our Tradition

rabbi meir, the peacemaker

This Talmudic story illustrates the extent to which Rabbi Meir would go to achieve peace between a husband and wife.

A man accused his wife of committing adultery with Rabbi Meir. In order to make peace between this man and his wife, Rabbi Meir allowed the woman to spit in his face in the presence of his students. When they protested that this was an insult to both Rabbi Meir and the Torah, Rabbi Meir replied, "Is it not enough that Meir's honor should be like that of his Creator? If the Holy Name, which is written in holiness, may be washed off into the water of bitterness in order to efface jealousy and make peace between a man and his wife (*Numbers,* 5.23), should this not apply all the more to the honor of Meir?" (*Leviticus Rabbah* 9)

Questions

1. If you were friends with a married couple who preferred not to accept help when they were having problems in their relationship, would you observe their wishes?

2. Reb Nahman once said that "When there is no peace, prayers are not heard." What do you think he meant by this statement?

3. The Talmud (*Gittin* 59b) says that "The whole Torah exists for the sake of peace, and for the sake of peace, even the truth may be sacrificed." Do you think that one should sacrifice truth for the sake of peace? Under what circumstances might this be appropriate?

aaron—peacemaker par excellence

Aaron has come to be known in Jewish tradition as the man of peace. This story illustrates the means by which Aaron worked to achieve peace.

When Aaron walked on the highway and was bothered by a wicked man, he would greet him cordially. The next day, if the wicked man wished to perform an evil deed, he thought to himself, "If I meet Aaron again and he greets me so cordially, how bad will I feel?" This way Aaron led the wicked man to refrain from doing wrong. When Aaron heard that two people had quarreled, he would go to one and say, "I have just come from the person whom you believe to be your enemy, and what have I seen? He beats at his heart and rends his garments and cries out, 'I have sinned against my neighbor. Woe is me. I am ashamed to look him in the face.'" Aaron would then do the same thing at the home of the other person. Thus, when the two men met again, they hugged and embraced.

Therefore, when Aaron died, the entire house of Israel wept for him, women as well as men. It was said, "So many married couples were reunited by Aaron after domestic quarrels that many thousands of families to whom a son was born named the child Aaron in his honor. At his death, eighty thousand persons named Aaron walked in the funeral procession"

(*Avot de Rabbi Natan* 12; Talmud, *Kallah* 3).

Questions

1. Have you ever interceded to help break up an argument? What are some of the best techniques to use?

2. According to the Talmud (*Gittin* 5.8), certain rules were laid down in the interest of keeping peace. In the interest of peace, it is considered robbery to seize something found by a a person who is deaf and mute, a person with mental

retardation or a minor, even though they are not legally considered competent in Jewish law. In the interest of peace, the poor of other religions may not be prevented from joining the Jewish poor in gathering gleanings, forgotten sheaves and grain left in the corner of a field. What rules would you institute in order to keep peace? Fill in the blanks.

In the interest of peace _____

In the interest of peace _____

3. Rav Hai Gaon once warned, "When people start to quarrel, leave them and do not get caught in their snares." What do you think of Rav Hai's approach? How do you decide when to get involved in a dispute and when not to get involved?

4. The Lubliner Rebbe once wrote, "Better an insincere peace than a sincere quarrel." What do you think he meant by this statement? Do you agree with it?

5. Research some of the prayers for peace in the prayerbook. What elements do they have in common?

11. a good name—shem tou

A good name is preferable to great riches (Proverbs, 22.1).

For Jewish people, a name is a complicated gift. Not only does it bestow identity, it can also reflect religious and spiritual dimensions. The Bible portrays naming as the first independent human act. It underscores the importance of names in its attention to dramatic name changes. For example, Jacob, after struggling with an angel, is given the name Israel, "champion of God." A "good name" refers to a person's reputation, and Jewish tradition generally stresses that a good name must be earned.

From Our Tradition

the value of a good name

This statement describes Yekhiel ben Yekutiel's understanding of the virtue of a good name. Yekutiel wrote *Sefer Ma'alot ha-Middot*, a thirteenth-century text about Jewish spiritual values and virtues.

> The virtue of a good name will come to a person as a result of work in service to God, and this is a very important virtue only found in the pious, people of accomplishment and those who fear God. Their good names travel far and wide. Even the Holy One strove to establish a good name in the universe, as it is written, "Who is like Your people Israel, a unique nation on earth, whom You went and redeemed as Your people, winning fame

for Yourself and doing great and wondrous deeds for them?" *(II Samuel, 7.23)* *(Ecclesiastes Rabbah 7.2)* *(Sefer Ma'alot ha-Middot)*

Questions

1. How does serving God lead to a good name?

2. There is an old saying, "Sticks and stones may break my bones, but names will never hurt me." Do you agree with this statement? Can names ever hurt a person?

3. Jews-by-choice often take the name of Abraham or Sarah as their Hebrew name. What is the reason for this custom?

4. Most people have nicknames. Do you have one? If so, why do people call you by your nickname? What is the purpose of nicknames?

leaving with a good name

This midrashic tale is a commentary on the verse in Ecclesiastes 7.1, "The day of death is better than the day of birth."

Rabbi Pinchas said, "When a person is born, all rejoice; when a person dies, all cry. It should not be so. When people are born there should be no rejoicing, because it is not known whether they will be righteous or wicked, good or bad. However, if a person departs the world in peace, with a good name, there is cause for rejoicing when that person dies. It is as if there were two ships, one leaving the harbor and the other entering it. As one sailed out of the harbor, all rejoiced, but no one displayed any joy over the ship that was entering the harbor. A shrewd man was there, and he said to the people, 'There is no reason to rejoice over the ship that is leaving the harbor, because nobody knows what its fate will be. But when it returns to the harbor, there is reason to rejoice, since it has come back safely'"

(*Ecclesiastes Rabbah* 7.1, 4).

Questions

1. What is the moral of the story of the two ships? Do you agree with the moral of this story?

2. *Pirke Avot* 1.13 tells us that "one who glorifies his own name will lose it." How does a person glorify his own name?

3. In 1953 the Israeli government established an institution called Yad Vashem in memory of Jews who died in the Holocaust. Look up Isaiah 56.5, from which the name Yad Vashem is derived. Why do you think that this Holocaust institution came to be called Yad Vashem?

4. The Talmud (*Brakhot* 57a) says that if a person dreams of sitting in a small boat, that person will acquire a good name. If a person dreams of sitting in a large boat, both that person and his or her family will acquire good names, but only if the boat is on the high seas. What do you think is the connection between boats and names?

12. honor——kavod

> The place does not honor the person;
> the person honors the place. *(Ta'anit 19b)*

Marks of distinction (in Hebrew, *kavod*) accorded to individuals are represented in Talmudic literature as tokens of self-respect or honor of self. The word *kavod* has been used to refer to the splendor of God, who is sometimes referred to in rabbinic literature as *Ha-Kavod*, the Glorious One. God imparts glory and splendor to those who revere God, especially the prophets and the righteous. Just as God bestows *kavod*, so Jews are commanded to show honor to worthy people.

It is natural for people to seek honor from their fellow human beings. However, the rabbis consistently warn that honor cannot be acquired by one who pursues it. In fact, the more one chases after an honor, the more elusive that honor becomes. Honor only pursues the person who seeks to avoid it.

From Our Tradition

sit toward the front

This story from the Talmud is intended to teach an important lesson about honor.

> Rav Nahman bar Isaac was seated among the young students. Rav Nahman bar Rav Hisda went to him and said, "Will you not be good enough to take a place more towards the front, where I am seated?"

Rav Naḥman bar Isaac replied, "The place does not honor the person, but the person honors the place. When the *Shekhinah* was on Mount Sinai, no one was allowed to approach the Mount, but when the *Shekhinah* departed, everyone was allowed to ascend it" (Talmud, *Taanit* 21b).

Questions

1. What is the moral of this story? Can you give examples of ways a person can honor a place?

2. It is said, "There is a respect people receive for themselves, and there is a respect people receive because they are intimate with someone who is respected" (*Tikkun Zohar* 12a). What do you think is meant by this statement?

3. *Pirke Avot* 4.1 says, "Who is honored? One who honors his fellow human beings." Complete this, "Who is honored? One who _____."

who shall enter first?

This tale from the Jerusalem Talmud concerns the protocol for giving honors to scholars of various abilities.

The family of Rav Oshaya and the family of Bar Pazi were often guests of the Patriarch. Rav Oshaya's family would enter first, because Rav Oshaya was the greater scholar. Later, when there was a matrimonial connection between the Patriarch and the Bar Pazi family, the latter wished to enter first.

Rabbi Ammi was questioned about this, and he said the relationship of Bar Pazi's family to the Patriarch placed them on an equal footing with Rav Oshaya's family. Therefore, Rav Oshaya's family should continue to enter first, as was the previous custom.

At another time, one family acted as political counselors to the Patriarch, and they entered first at his receptions. Another family contained several scholars, and they wished to be allowed to take precedence. Rabbi Yoḥanan decreed that the scholarly family should be granted the right to enter first, since a scholar ranks above a politician (Jerusalem Talmud, *Shabbat* 12).

Questions

1. What do you think of the protocol regarding honors in a family? Do you think scholars ought to be treated differently than other people? Do you think honors should be granted according to a scholar's rank? Why?

2. According to the *Code of Jewish Law* (*Yoreh Deah* 244.15), students should honor their teachers by rising in their presence. What is your opinion of this suggestion? What are some things that students today can do to honor their teachers?

3. Proverbs 3.9, says that one should "honor God with one's wealth." What do you think this means?

13. wealth——osher

Ben Zoma said, "Who is rich? People who are
happy with what they have." *(Pirke Avot, 4.1)*.

Judaism has always had a relatively positive view of wealth,
and the Talmud is replete with sayings that denounce the nega-
tive effects of poverty. The rabbis said, "Poverty is one of the
three things that drive a person out of one's mind" (Talmud, *Eruvin*
41b). It is a religious obligation to provide properly for oneself
and one's family. It is equally an obligation to share one's wealth
with others and to thank God for one's bounty.

Rabbinic sources also point to the dangers of amassing too
much wealth, reminding us that it was no accident that the calf
the Israelites fashioned in the wilderness was made of gold.
Hillel used to say that the more possessions one had, the greater
one's anxiety *(Pirke Avot 2.8)*. The accumulation of too much wealth
can increase one's worries about loss, robbery and theft. That
is why Ben Zoma said that the rich are those people who are
happy with what they have *(Pirke Avot 4.1)*.

From Our Tradition
prayer for the congregation

The following prayer, generally recited on the Sabbath and
festivals, was composed in late Talmudic times, and it sums up
our concerns for the whole community.

May God who blessed our ancestors, Abraham, Isaac
and Jacob, Sarah, Rebecca, Rachel and Leah, bless this

69

entire congregation, together with all holy congregations, them, their sons and daughters, their families and all that is theirs, along with those who unite to establish synagogues for prayer and those who enter them to pray, and those who give funds for heat and light and wine for Kiddush and Havdalah, bread to the wayfarer and charity to the poor, and all who devotedly involve themselves with the needs of this community and the Land of Israel. May the Holy Blessed One reward them. May God remove sickness from them, heal them and forgive their sins. May God bless them by prospering all their worthy endeavors, as well as those of the entire people Israel, and let us say, Amen.

Questions

1. According to this prayer, what material things does the community need? If you were to rewrite this prayer, what would you request for your community?

2. In the name of Rabbah bar Rav Adda, the Talmud (*Kiddushin* 70a) said, "Whoever marries a woman for her riches will have worthless children." What do you think he meant by this statement?

3. The Talmud (*Bava Batra* 175b) says, "One who wishes to acquire wisdom should study the way money works, for there is no greater area of Torah study than this." How does money work? In what way can this kind of knowledge lead to the acquisition of wisdom?

4. In the Talmud (*Tamid* 32b) we are told that Alexander the Great was given an eyeball. He weighed all of his silver and gold against it but found they were not equal to it. He said to the rabbis, "How is this possible?"

They answered, "It is the eyeball of a human being, and this is why they are never satisfied." What do you think is meant by this short tale?

the betrothal of akiba and kalba savu'a's daughter

This Talmudic tale describes the extreme poverty of a married couple and a lesson that is taught to them by Elijah the Prophet.

The daughter of the wealthy landowner Kalba Savu'a betrothed herself to Rabbi Akiba, who was just a poor shepherd at the time. When her father heard of the betrothal, he vowed never to give a cent of his money or property to her.

The couple was married in the winter, and they were so poor that they had to sleep on straw.

"If only I could afford it," Akiba told his wife as he picked straw from her hair, "I would give you a golden ornament with a picture of Jerusalem on it."

One day the prophet Elijah came to visit them, disguised as a mortal. "Give me some straw," he cried out at their door. "My wife is about to give birth, and I have nothing for her to lie on."

"You see," said Akiba to his wife. "We think we are poor; there is a person who does not even have straw"

(Talmud, *Nedarim* 50a).

Questions

1. What is the moral of this story? What is Rabbi Akiba's definition of wealth?

2. Rabbi Yosi once said, "Respect other people's money as much as you do your own" (Talmud, *Pirke Avot* 2.17). What do you think this means?

3. The Jerusalem Talmud (*Terumot* 8) says, "All the members of the body depend on the heart, and the heart depends on the purse." What does this mean?

4. In the Bible (Genesis 28.20-22) Jacob makes the following vow to God. "If God will be with me and keep me on this journey I am making, and give me bread to eat and clothes to put on...then shall God be my God...and of all that You shall give me, I will give to You one tenth." What is your opinion of Jacob's conditional vow? What does this kind of vow tell us about human nature?

14. taking care of the body—shmirat ha-guf

Anyone who sits around idly and takes no exercise will be subject to physical discomforts and failing strength
(*Code of Jewish Law*, Abridged Version, chapter 31).

According to the rabbinic view, God is the owner of everything, including our bodies. God loans bodies to people for the duration of their lives and takes them back at the time of death. If God owns our bodies, then we are obligated to care for those bodies by practicing good hygiene, getting enough sleep, exercising and following a healthy diet. Deuteronomy sums up Judaism's attitude about caring for one's body when it says, "Take good heed of your souls" (Deuteronomy 4.15).

From Our Tradition

rabbi hillel and the bathhouse

In the course of the following conversation, Hillel makes the point to his pupils that one must not only be concerned about knowledge and intellect, but also about the care of one's body.

The story is told of Hillel that when he had completed a lesson with his students, he accompanied them part of the way. They said to him, "Master, where are you going?"

He answered, "To perform a mitzvah."

They asked, "Which mitzvah?"

He responded, "To bathe in the bathhouse."

They questioned, "Is that a mitzvah?"

He answered them, "If someone is appointed to scrape and clean the statues of the king that are set up in the theaters and circuses, and is paid to do the work, and furthermore associates with the nobility, how much more so should I, who am created in the Divine image and likeness, take care of my body?" (*Leviticus Rabbah* 34.3)

Questions

1. What basic tenet of Jewish thought does this story attempt to teach? How does it compare with the Greco-Roman view of the body?

2. The idea that the body is a creation of God, and its pleasures are God-given and ought to be used as a source of holiness, is a major principle in Jewish medical ethics. What are some ways in which a Jew can use his or her body for attaining holiness?

3. Can you think of other mitzvot that concern the body in some way? See if there are any common attitudes in the list that you compile.

4. In the Talmud (*Avodah Zarah* 20a), the story is told that Rabban Shimon ben Gamliel was standing on the Temple steps when he saw an extraordinarily beautiful pagan woman walk by. He said, "How great are Your works, O God" (Psalms 104.24). What do you think his purpose was in reciting this verse from the Book of Psalms? Research the blessing Jews are commanded to recite when seeing beautiful living things. What is the blessing, and what is its purpose?

prayer for our body

The following is a prayer that appears in the very earliest part of the preliminary morning service.

> Praised are You, Adonai our God, Ruler of the universe, Who has with wisdom created humanity and has fashioned them with openings and passageways. It is revealed and known before Your holy throne that if just one of these were perforated or obstructed, it would be impossible to survive before You. Praised are You, Adonai, who heals all creatures and does wonders (Prayer *Asher Yatzar*).

Questions

1. What is the theme of this prayer? What experience do you think inspired the writer to compose the prayer? Have you ever had a similar experience?

2. Some people have been known to refer to this prayer as the bathroom prayer. Can you guess why?

3. On what occasions do you think it might be appropriate to recite this prayer?

4. Jewish tradition forbids the cremation of a body. Why?

5. Leviticus 19.28 says that one should not make any tattoo marks on oneself. Why do you think some people would make tattoo marks on their flesh? Why do you think the Torah forbids this practice?

6. What does the concept of being created in God's image remind you to do?

15. compassion——rahamim

You shall not wrong a stranger or oppress him, for
you were strangers in the land of Egypt. You shall not
mistreat any widow or orphan (Exodus 22.20-21).

The Torah has always understood how much a part of
human nature it is to take advantage of society's weakest
people. Such marginal members of society would include the
elderly, the bereaved, those seeking political asylum in a new
land, the poor, the weak, widows and orphans, the homeless,
people with physical disabilities and the sick. Thus the Torah is
filled with commandments related to helping these people. For
instance, concerning the stranger it states, "You shall not wrong
a stranger or oppress him" (Exodus 22.20). The Torah claims that
strangers are the sole category of people whom God is identified
as loving. The Bible says, "And God loves the stranger."

A traditional prayer in the beginning of the Passover
Haggadah says "Let all who are hungry come and eat, let all
who are needy come and make Passover."

Caring for the dead and the bereaved is another important
Jewish religious obligation. Showing compassion to the bereaved in their time of pain and loss can be very important to
their healing process.

From Our Tradition

moses sees his brothers' burdens

The following midrash is meant to explain and elaborate on Exodus 2.11, which says that "when Moses went out to look upon his brothers, he saw their burdens."

> "And when Moses went out to look upon his brothers, he saw their burdens (Exodus 2.11)." How did he feel when he looked upon them? As he looked at their burdens, he cried, saying, "Woe is me for your servitude. Would that I could die for you." Since no work is more strenuous than that of handling clay, Moses used to shoulder the burden and help each worker.
>
> Rabbi Eleazar, the son of Rabbi Yosi the Galilean, said, "He saw heavy burdens put upon small people and light ones on big people; men's burdens on women, and women's burdens on men; the burden an older person could carry placed on a youth, and the burden of a youth on an older person. So Moses would from time to time step away from his retinue and rearrange the burdens, pretending that he was really trying to be of help to Pharaoh. The Holy One said, 'You left your own concerns and went to look compassionately at the distress of Israel, behaving like a brother to them. So, I too, will leave those on high and those below, and speak only with you'" (Exodus Rabbah 1.27-28).

Questions

1. Why does the midrash elaborate upon the verse in Exodus and explain in detail the extent to which Moses helped his fellow workers?

2. The Hebrew word for compassion is *rahmanut*, which has the same root as the Hebrew word *rehem*, meaning "womb." Can you see a connection between the two words that would better explain the Jewish view of compassion?

3. One of God's many rabbinic names is *Rahmana*, the Compassionate One. Can you think of a time when God showed compassion to you or someone you love?

4. According to Rabbi Nahman of Bretslav, when there is no compassion, crime increases. Do you agree?
Complete this sentence. When there is no compassion, there is _____.

two donkey drivers

This midrashic story describes two donkey drivers who greatly disliked each other and how the recognition of a verse from the Torah brought them closer together.

Rabbi Alexandri said, "Two donkey drivers who hated each other were walking on a road when one of the donkeys collapsed under its burden. The other driver saw this but continued on his way. But then he reflected, "Does the Torah not say, 'If you see the donkey of one who hates you lying flat under its load and your inclination is to refrain from raising it, you must nevertheless raise it with him'" (Exodus 23.5)?

So he returned and helped his enemy to raise the donkey and rearrange the load. He began talking to his enemy, "Loosen it a little here. Pull a bit tighter here. Unload over there."

Before long peace developed between the two of them, so that the driver of the unloaded donkey reflected, "I thought he hated me, but look how compassionate he was." By and by the two entered an inn, ate and drank together and became friends. Why did they make peace and become friends? Because one of them kept what was written in the Torah, "You have established harmony" (Psalms 99.4) (*Tanhuma, Mishpatim* 1).

Questions

1. What is the moral of the story of the two donkey drivers?

2. What are some of the opportunities for compassion that present themselves every day?

3. There is an interesting quotation in the Talmud (*Brakhot* 7a) that suggests that God prays. This is God's prayer: "May My attribute of compassion overcome My attribute of harsh justice." What can people learn from God's prayer?

4. What are some of the ways that people can demonstrate compassion toward animals?

16. slow to anger— erekh apayim

An angry person cannot be a teacher (*Pirke Avot* 2.6).

The rabbis say that life is not worth living if one is quick to anger, since one is always miserable, regretting the hurtful things one says in anger and the harm one causes others. The rabbis went so far as to point out that when Moses lost his temper, his wisdom departed from him.

God's slowness to anger is referred to throughout the Torah. As a matter of fact, the virtue of being slow to anger is first mentioned as one of God's thirteen attributes (Exodus 34.6). Calm and serenity are considered virtues in Judaism. Since life brings with it so many stressful situations, a person must work diligently to control anger.

From Our Tradition
rabbi hillel and the wager

In this Talmudic tale, a man makes a wager that Hillel, known for his gentleness, can be made to lose his temper.

> A man once bet his friend that he could make Hillel lose his temper. If the man succeeded, he was to receive four hundred *zuzim*, but if he failed, he was to forfeit this sum. The Shabbat eve was approaching, and Hillel was engaged in his personal washing when

a man passing his door shouted, "Where is Hillel?" Wrapping his robe about him, Hillel sallied forth to ask what the man wanted.

"I wish to ask you a question" was the reply.

"Ask, my son," said Hillel.

"I wish to know why the Babylonians have such round heads," said the man.

"A very important question, my man," said Hillel. "The reason is that their midwives were not clever."

Several times this procedure was repeated. "I have many more inquiries, but you will lose patience with me and become angry," said the questioner.

"Ask what you wish," answered Hillel.

The man, in annoyance, said, "May there not be many like you in Israel, O Chief Justice. Through you I have lost four hundred *zuzim* on a wager that I would make you lose your temper."

"Be warned for the future," said Hillel. "Better it is that you should lose four hundred *zuzim* and four hundred more after them than have it said of Hillel that he lost his temper" (Talmud, Shabbat 31a).

Questions

1. Have you ever come close to losing your temper but at the last moment thought better of it? What can you suggest to a person who has difficulty controlling his or her temper?

2. What did the man in the story do to try to make Hillel angry? Why do you think it was so important to Hillel not to lose his temper?

3. In Exodus 34.6 the words "slow to anger" are sandwiched in between the words "compassionate" and "gracious" in the description of God's thirteen attributes. What is the connection between being compassionate and being slow to anger?

4. Proverbs 16.32 says that it is "better to be slow to anger than mighty, to have self-control than to conquer a city." Do you agree with this teaching?

5. The Talmud, *Brakhot* 29, says, "Do not grow angry, and you will not sin." Do you agree with this advice?

the four temperaments

People differ in tendencies and personalities. This brief description from *Pirke Avot* 5.13 attempts to describe different categories of temperaments.

There are four types of temperaments.
Easy to anger and easy to appease—the loss is cancelled by the reward.
Hard to anger and hard to appease—the reward is cancelled by the loss.
Easy to anger and hard to appease—a wicked person.
Hard to anger and easy to appease—a saintly person

(Pirke Avot 5.13).

Questions

1. Which of the above temperaments describes you? Are you happy with the temperament that you have? If not, what kind of changes would you like to make?

2. Rabbi Simeon ben Levi said, "A sage who indulges in anger loses his knowledge" (Talmud, *Pesaḥim* 66a). What do you think he meant by this statement? Do you agree with it?

3. The Talmud, *Eruvin* 65b, says that "...character can be judged by the way a person handles three things: drink, money and anger." What do you think is meant by this statement? Do you agree with it? If you were to describe how a person's character can be judged, how would you fill in the blanks?

   Character can be judged by the way a person handles

   _____.

4. How would you advise someone to handle a situation in which he is provoked to anger?

17. truthfulness——emet

The seal of God is truth (Talmud, *Shabbat* 55a).

"The seal of the Holy Blessed One is truth" (Talmud, *Shabbat* 55a). This saying epitomizes Judaism's regard for truth and honesty. In addition to truthfulness in the ethical and moral sphere, rabbinic thinkers also emphasize the need for intellectual honesty. Almost all Talmudic debates are founded on the need to arrive at the truth by carefully examining the evidence and seeing where it leads. The ability to acknowledge the truth is one of the seven characteristics of a wise person listed in *Pirke Avot* 5.9.

Without truth, society and human relationships simply cannot endure. A customer making a purchase must be able to trust the seller. A homeowner has to assume that the person making a home repair will do his best work. A client has to believe his lawyer. A patient has to trust his doctor. Unless people are honest, our most basic relationships will disintegrate.

From Our Tradition

truth prevents crimes

The following tale describes how a vow to tell the truth prevents a crime from being perpetrated.

> A young man came into the presence of Simeon ben Shetah and said, "I find it difficult to control my evil inclinations. What shall I do?"
>
> Simeon answered, "Swear to me that you will always tell the truth. Then you will be cured." The youth uttered

the vow but wondered at the lightness of Simeon's injunction.

However, once he entered a neighbor's home while she was away and stole her valuables. A few moments later he thought to himself, "If all of the neighbors are questioned, I will be included, and I swore to tell the truth." He quickly worked to restore and return the stolen goods, and he then appreciated the wisdom of Simeon's counsel (*Midrash ha-Katzar* in *Rav Pealim*).

Questions

1.   Do you think it is a good idea to vow always to tell the truth? Do you think you could do it?

2.   According to the midrash on Psalms 118, after we die, each of us will stand in judgment before God and be asked four questions before entering the Gates of Righteousness. The first question is "Were you honest in your business dealings?" Does this question surprise you? What does it tell us about the importance of honesty?

3.   A woman is told by a doctor that her spouse is dying of a life-threatening illness. The patient has a maximum of six months to live under optimal conditions. There are no medical means available to either extend his life span or cure the disease. In your view, should the patient be told the true nature of the illness? What values come into play in making this decision?

casting truth upon the ground

The following midrash deals with the question of whether it is always best to tell the truth, especially in a situation where truth conflicts with other values.

> Rabbi Simon said, When God was about to create Adam, the ministering angels split into contending groups. Some said, "Let him be created," while others cried, "Let him not be created." That is why it is written, "Mercy and truth collided, righteousness and peace engaged in a clash" (Psalm 85.11).
>
> Mercy said, "Let people be created, for they will do merciful deeds." Truth said, "Let people not be created, for they will lie."
>
> What did the Holy Blessed One do? God took truth and cast it to the ground (*Genesis Rabbah* 8.5).

Questions

1. What does this midrash teach us about the value of truth? Under what circumstances do you think the truth can be set aside in favor of another value? Why did truth have to be cast to the ground before people could be created?

2. The Talmud, *Brakhot,* advises, "Teach your tongue to say 'I do not know,' lest you invent something and be trapped." What is the meaning of this suggestion? Do you agree with it?

3. The rabbis occasionally permitted white lies, especially those intended to promote peace and harmony. Can you think of an occasion when you altered the truth for the sake of peace?

4. The Talmud (*Bava Metzia* 23b-24a) observes that a scholar will never tell a lie except about tractate, bed and hospitality. The commentators explain "tractate" to mean that a modest scholar is permitted to declare that he is unfamiliar with a tractate of the Mishnah in order not to flaunt his learning. "Bed" is understood to mean that if a person is asked to answer intimate questions regarding his marital life, he need not answer truthfully. "Hospitality" is understood to mean that a person who has been generously treated by a host may decide not to tell the truth about his reception if he fears that as a result the host will be embarrassed by unwelcome guests.

    Can you think of instances when it might be appropriate to tell a lie? What is your opinion of the observation of the Talmud?

5. You see your brother taking ten dollars from your dad's wallet. At dinner, your father angrily tells the family that in the morning he is going to dismiss the cleaning woman for stealing money from his wallet. Your brother is silent on the matter. What would you do?

18. not coveting——lo tahmod

> The person who is envious is guilty of robbery in
> thought (Nahman of Bretslav).

The only one of the Ten Commandments that deals with a
person's feelings and emotions is the one related to envy. The
Torah tells us, "You shall not be jealous of your neighbor's
house, or field, or servant, or anything that belongs to your
neighbor" (*Exodus* 20.14). In Judaism, envy is usually described as
taking one of two forms. In the first form, a person casts an
envious eye upon the possessions (husband or wife, home and
so forth) of another person, but his envy does not go beyond
daydreaming. Although such envy is forbidden, these feelings
are not subject to penalty, because they represent a violation of
Jewish law in thought but not in deed. The second form is the
envy that leads to action. This kind of coveting involves not
only a desire for the possessions of another, but also devious attempts to talk the other person into giving up his possessions.
The only kind of envy that the rabbinic authorities not only
tolerate but advocate is envy of those who study the Torah and
practice its laws. Thus, one of their favorite sayings was, "The
envy of scholars increases wisdom" (Talmud, *Bava Batra* 21).

From Our Tradition
prayer for contentment

The following is a prayer that is found in the Jerusalem
Talmud.

May it be Your will, O Eternal my God and God of my ancestors, that no hatred against any person come into our hearts and no hatred against us come into the hearts of any person, and may no one be jealous of us, and may we not be jealous of any. May Your law be our labor all the days of our lives, and may our words be as petitions before You (Jerusalem Talmud, *Brakhot* 4.2).

Questions

1. What is the gist of this prayer? Would you ever wish to include it in your daily regimen of prayers?

2. Do you think it is fair to command a person not to be envious, since it is part of human nature to be desirous of something that someone else possesses?

3. According to the midrash (*Genesis Rabbah* 9.9), "Without envy, the world could not abide, for then no one would marry or build a house." What do you think the midrash is trying to tell us? Do you agree?

4. The Talmud (*Shabbat* 152b) says, "When people have envy in their heart, their bones rot, but when they have no envy in their heart, their bones do not rot." Why do you think that envy is compared to rotten bones?

simeon ben gamaliel's advice

Rabbi Simeon ben Gamaliel said, "He who makes peace in his house, the Bible reckons it as if he made peace for every single Israelite in Israel. He who brings jealousy and strife into his house, as if he brought them among all Israel" (*Avot de Rabbi Natan* 28.43).

Questions

1. In your own words, what advice is Simeon ben Gamaliel giving to us? Do you agree with it?

2. The Songs of Songs says that "jealousy is as cruel as the grave." What is meant by this?

3. Rabbi Elazar HaKappar taught, "Envy, lust and pursuit of honor will ruin a person's life" (*Pirke Avot,* 4.28). How might envy ruin a person's life?

4. The last of the Ten Commandments tells us not to be jealous. Why do you think that God placed this last on the list? What is the relationship between covetousness and the other nine commandments?

19. using good words— lashon ha-tov

Keep your tongue from speaking evil, and your lips from speaking deceit (Prayer book).

Normally, when one thinks of ethics, one thinks about how people's actions affect those around them. In Judaism, how people's words affect those around them is also an ethical issue. Words can be powerful. When used properly, words can soothe, comfort and bless. When used improperly they can hurt, injure and curse. The power of words was proclaimed in biblical times in the well-known warning, "Death and life are in the power of the tongue" (*Proverbs* 18.21).

From Our Tradition

the power of the tongue

This midrashic tale is intended to teach the importance of speech and the power of words.

> One of the ancient rabbis sent his servant to the market with the general instruction, "Buy the best thing there that one can eat." The servant returned with a tongue.

> Later, the rabbi asked him to go back to the market to buy the worst thing that one could eat. The servant again came back with a tongue.

"What is it with you?" asked the rabbi. "I have asked you to buy both the best and the worst, and you come back with a couple of tongues."

"That is true," responded the servant. "After all, cannot a tongue be one of the best things in the world and one of the worst?" (*Leviticus Rabbah* 33)

Questions

1. What unethical things can words do?

2. The Hebrew word for words is *devarim*. The Hebrew word for bees is *devorim*. What is the connection between these two words?

3. The Talmud (*Ketubot* 5a-b) says, "If you hear something unseemly, put your hands on your ears." What is your opinion of this advice? What do you personally do if you hear something unseemly?

4. A great many so-called obscene words deal with parts of the body or bodily functions. Why do you think there is this connection?

5. How do you feel about censorship in the recording industry? Are you offended by the language used in some songs today?

gather the feathers

This Hasidic folktale attempts to explain the dire effects of words that slander another person.

A man would often slander his rabbi until one day, feeling remorse, he begged for forgiveness and indicated that he was willing to undergo any penance to make amends. The rabbi told him to take several pillows from his home, cut them open and scatter the feathers to the winds. The man did so immediately and returned to the rabbi to notify him that he had fulfilled his request. The rabbi then told him, "Go and gather all the feathers that the wind has scattered. For though you are sincerely remorseful and truly desirous of correcting the evil you have done, it is as possible to repair the damage done by your words as it will be to recover the feathers (Hasidic folktale).

Questions

1. What is the moral of this Hasidic tale? What is there about slander that makes it such a great crime?

2. According to the Jerusalem Talmud, "Hot coals that are cooled on the outside grow cool within, but gossip and slander, even if cooled outwardly, do not cool inwardly" (Jerusalem Talmud, *Peah* 1.1). What is meant by this statement?

3. Research the *Al Het* confession that is recited on Yom Kippur. Identify those sins that deal with language. Why do you think so many of them deal with communication?

4. During a radio broadcast a political writer once remarked, "We have to use words to talk the same way as we use cooking utensils to cook." What does this statement mean to you?

5. We generally elect our public officials to office on the basis of their speeches. By what criteria ought we to judge a person's words?

6. A Hasidic teaching states that "human beings are God's language." Try to explain this expression.

20. work-industriousness—melakhah

God took man and put him into the Garden of Eden
to till and tend it (Genesis, 2.15).

Work is every person's God-given duty, and Judaism has always stressed the importance of productive work. A person who works is able to be self-supporting. The rabbis taught that, in addition to teaching their children Torah, parents must teach their children trades or professions (Talmud, *Kiddushin* 29a). Study, the rabbis insisted, cannot be complete when divorced from the world of active work.

The Bible itself has always exalted work and industriousness. In the opening chapters of the book of Genesis, God is portrayed as a laborer. When God created the first human being, man was told to work and till the soil. Just as the Torah was given to people as a covenant, so too work was given as a covenant, as it is said, "Six days you shall labor and do all of your work, but the seventh day is the Sabbath of the Lord your God" (Exodus 20.9).

From Our Tradition

living from the labor of his hands

This rabbinic passage from the Talmudic tractate *Brakhot* 8a praises work and the happiness that results from industriousness.

A man who lives from the labor of his hands is greater than the one who fears heaven. For with regard to the one who fears heaven it is written, "Happy is the man who fears God" (Psalms 112.1). With regard to the man who lives from his own work, it is written, "When you eat the labor of your hands, happy shall you be, and it shall be well with you" (Psalm 128.2). This means "Happy shall you be" in this world, "and it shall be well with you" in the world to come. But of the person who fears heaven it is also written, "and it shall be well with you" (Talmud, *Brakhot* 8a).

Questions

1. What is this passage trying to teach us? What does the passage use to prove its point?

2. The midrash (Psalms 23.3) says, "If a person works, that person is blessed." How does a person's work relate to receiving a blessing?

3. The Jerusalem Talmud (Pea<u>h</u> 1) says, "Choose life, namely a trade." What do you think this statement means?

4. A man lamented to his rabbi, "I am frustrated that my work leaves me no time for study or prayer."

   The rabbi replied, "Perhaps your work is more pleasing to God than study or prayer" (<u>H</u>asidic tale). What do you think the rabbi meant? In what way can one's work be more pleasing to God than study or prayer?

first work, then reward

This tale from *Avot de Rabbi Natan* 11, 23a tells of the connection between work and reward.

Rabbi Simeon ben Elazar said, "Even Adam did not taste food until he had done work, as it is said, 'The Eternal God took the man, and put him in the Garden to till and keep it' *(Genesis, 2.15)*, after which God said, 'Of every tree of the garden you may eat'" *(Genesis, 2.16)*.

Rabbi Tarfon said, "Even the Holy Blessed One did not have the Shekhina to rest upon Israel until they had done work, as it is said, 'Let them make for me a sanctuary, and then I will dwell among them *(Exodus, 25.8)*'" *(Avot de Rabbi Natan 11, 23a)*.

Questions

1. What reward does Adam receive from working the land? What reward do the Israelites get for completing the sanctuary?

2. Is there work today that has spiritual rewards?

3. *Pirke Avot* says, "You are not obliged to complete the work, neither are you free to desist from working at it." What does this statement mean to you?

4. What examples of pride in work do you see in your local community?

5. The Talmud *(Megillah 6a)* contains this interesting statement about work: "If a person says to you, 'I have worked and have not achieved,' do not believe that person. If the person says, 'I have not worked, but still I have achieved,' do not believe that person. But if the person says, 'I have worked and I have achieved,' you may believe that person." What is the Talmud trying to teach us? Do you agree with the teaching?

21. not embarrassing— lo levayesh

> The destruction of Jerusalem resulted from the humiliation of Bar Kamtza (Talmud, Gittin 55b-56a).

Ideas of what constitutes shame have changed over time. According to Solomon ibn Gabirol, the best of the ten virtues that God gave us is a sense of shame. This explains the Talmudic dictum. Jerusalem was destroyed because its inhabitants had no shame (Talmud, *Shabbat* 119b).

On the other hand, we are told that the sin of putting another person to shame in public is one of the gravest crimes. "Let a person throw him or herself into a blazing furnace rather than shame a fellow human being in public" (Talmud, *Brakhot* 43b). The Talmud (*Bava Metzia* 58b) says, "Shaming a fellow human being in public is like shedding blood."

From Our Tradition
the unauthorized man

This Talmudic tale discusses Samuel ha-Katon's desire to protect a person from shame.

Once Rabban Gamliel addressed the members of his court, "Choose from your group six people to come to my attic at sunrise to discuss whether the year shall have an additional month."

In the morning, he found seven persons beside him. He asked, "Who came unselected?"

Samuel ha-Katan arose and said, "I came to learn, not to take part."

An inquiry showed that Samuel had been selected. He said he had not been selected in order to protect the unauthorized person from humiliation.

This teaches that it is better to delay a mitzvah than to bring shame upon anyone (Talmud, *Sanhedrin* 11).

Questions

1. What do you think of Samuel ha-Katan's actions? Do you know people today who would do what he did in order to protect another person from being shamed?

2. The Jerusalem Talmud, *Brakhot* 4.2, says, "The gift of flesh and blood is little, but their shame is great." What is meant by this statement?

3. According to the Talmud (*Sanhedrin* 11a), it once happened that while Judah the Prince was lecturing he noticed a garlic smell. He said, "Let the one who has eaten garlic go out." Hiyya arose and left, and then all of the other disciples arose and they too went out. What is the moral of this story?

4. Why is shaming a person publicly so much more significant than shaming a person privately?

another's shame

This brief Talmudic tale, featuring Rabbis Huna and H̲ana bar H̲anilai, is intended to teach us another lesson about shame.

> Rav Huna was carrying an ax on his shoulder. Rav H̲ana bar H̲anilai came and sought to carry the ax himself.
>
> Rav Huna remarked, "If you carry such a tool for yourself, you may show me respect by taking it on your own shoulder, but if you do not do so for yourself, I do not wish to be honored by another's shame" (Talmud, *Bava Batra* 22).

Questions

1. What is the moral of this story?

2. According to the Talmud (*Bava Metzia* 59a), the person who whitens a comrade's face by publicly shaming him has no share in the world to come. Why do you think that the Talmud is making such a forceful statement here? Do you think this is just a powerful metaphor, or did the rabbis truly believe there was a real connection between shaming another publicly and being denied a place in the future world?

3. In the prayer *Ahavah Rabbah* we are told, "Open our eyes to Your help, and help our hearts to cleave to Your mitzvot. Unite all our thoughts to love and revere You. Then shall we never be brought to shame." How do you think Torah and mitzvot can save a person from shame? What else might a person do to protect himself from experiencing shame?

4. Rabbi Zeira's disciples once asked, "By what virtue have you reached such a ripe old age?"

    He answered, "I have never rejoiced in my neighbor's shame" (Talmud, *Taanit* 20b). What do you think is meant by this statement?

22. being pleasant—
sayver panim yafot

Be the first to greet every human being (Pirke Avot 4.20).

Everyone loves a person who is pleasant and always seems to show warmth and friendliness. *Pirke Avot* 1.15 advises, "Greet every person in a cheerful manner." Having a pleasant demeanor suggests a certain attitude toward people. Ideally, it involves greeting a person in an affable, gracious and congenial way. People who tend to possess this virtue are the kind of people who tend to have many friends. They are the kind of people toward whom others tend to gravitate.

From Our Tradition
the man who greets those who despise him

This tale describes Joseph's ability to greet his brothers in a friendly manner, even though he knew they disliked him immensely and would likely not respond to his greeting.

> Joseph's brothers hated him and would not return his greeting (*Genesis* 37.4). Joseph used to greet them, but they would not answer him. It was always his custom to greet them. Before they rise to greatness, some people will always greet other people, but when they achieve greatness, their spirit becomes pompous and they pay no attention to greeting their fellow citizens. Joseph was different. After he had risen to greatness, he still greeted

others (*Genesis* 43.27). God said to him, "Joseph, because you greeted your brothers in this world even though they hated you, I will reconcile you in the world to come and remove hatred from among you and settle you in friendship." As it is written, "How good it is when brothers dwell together in peace" (Psalm 133.1) (*Tanḥuma, Vayeshev* 90b).

Questions

1. Do you think it is possible to be like Joseph and greet one's siblings knowing that they literally despise you? Should prominent people have a special obligation to greet their fellow citizens?

2. What is the advantage of being a person who always has a pleasant demeanor? Do you know such people?

3. One verse of the Priestly Blessing (Numbers 6.25) says, "May God's face shine on you." What do you think this means? How does a person know when God's face shines on him or her? What is meant by "the face of God"?

4. What kind of facial expressions are associated with someone who is always sullen and unpleasant?

5. In your opinion, must a person maintain a pleasant demeanor even if he or she is feeling low?

faces

This brief passage from *Avot de Rabbi Natan* 13, 29a teaches the difference between having a pleasant demeanor and an unpleasant one.

If you give your fellow human being all of the best gifts in the world with a crabby face, Scripture regards it as if you had given the person nothing.

But when you receive your fellow person with a cheerful demeanor, Scripture credits you as though you have given the person all of the very best gifts in the entire world (*Avot de Rabbi Natan* 13, 29a).

Questions

1. What does this story this story teach us? How does one's demeanor affect the gifts that one gives to another person?

2. The *Book of Ecclesiastes*, 8.1, says that "...wisdom lights up a person's face, replacing the face of deep discontentment." What does this statement mean to you? Have you ever seen wisdom in a person's face?

3. Are you the type of person who greets a person before being greeted by that person? What are the advantages to greeting a person first?

4. Can making an effort to give people a warm and cheerful greeting help you to become a more pleasant person in general?

23. reverence for god— yirat ha-el

Reverence for God is the beginning of wisdom (Psalms 111.10).

No term has been used more often to express the roots of Jewish piety than *yirat ha-El*, reverence for God, and its rabbinic parallel *yirat shamayim,* fear of Heaven. True morality must be based on a right relation to God. In his *Mishnah Torah* (*Yesodai ha-Torah* 2.2), Maimonides describes true piety in the following terms. When a person contemplates God's great and wondrous works and obtains a glimpse of God's incomparable and infinite wisdom, that person will straightaway love and glorify God.

Some Jewish thinkers emphasize the general sense of *yirat ha-El* as sufficient reason for avoiding sin. "Antigonos of Socho used to say, 'Be like servants who serve the master without the expectation of receiving a reward, and let the fear of God simply bring you to it'" (*Pirke Avot* 1.3).

The Torah and all its wisdom and commandments rest on our *yirat ha-El*. Without it we lose Judaism's critical foundation. With it we embrace this well-known vision of *Ecclesiastes* 12.13, "The end of the matter, all having been heard. Fear God and keep God's commandments, for that is why you were created as a human being."

From Our Tradition

the loss of the queen's bracelet

This tale from the Jerusalem Talmud teaches an important lesson about the fear of God.

> Rav Samuel went to Rome shortly after the queen lost her bracelet. He found it. A crier went through the kingdom and said, "Whoever returns the bracelet within thirty days shall receive a reward, but if it is found upon him after thirty days, his head shall be cut off."

> Rav Samuel did not return the bracelet within thirty days, but he did return the bracelet on the thirty-first day. The queen said to the rabbi, "Haven't you been in the kingdom?"

> He answered, "Yes, I have."

> She said, "Have you not heard the proclamation?"

> He replied, "Yes, I have."

> She then said, "What did the crier say?"

> Rav Samuel told the queen what the crier had said. She asked, "So why did you not return the bracelet within thirty days?"

> He answered, "So that you should not say I returned the bracelet because I feared you, but because I feared God."

> The queen said, "Blessed be the God of the Jews"

(Jerusalem Talmud, *Bava Metzia* 11.5).

Questions

1. What is the moral of this story? Why did the queen say a blessing?

2. *Pirke Avot* 3.11 states, "One whose dread of sin precedes his/her wisdom, his/her wisdom shall endure." What does this statement mean to you?

3. The Talmud (*Shabbat* 31b) says that, "A person who possesses learning without reverence for God is like the person who has been entrusted with the keys of an inner court but not with the keys of the outer court. How is this person to enter?" What is the meaning of this statement? What is the connection between learning and piety?

the story of the waves

This Talmudic tale is meant to teach the importance of fearing God.

Rabbah related what certain sailors once told him: "Once we were on a journey, and a wave lifted us up until we saw where the smallest of the stars rests. Then there was a flash as if someone had shot forty iron arrows. Had the waves lifted us up any higher, we surely would have burned up from the heat. Then one wave called to his friend, "Did you leave behind anything in the world that you did not wash away? I will go and destroy it." The other wave replied, "Go and you will see the power of the Master by Whose injunction I must not go beyond the sand by even as little as a thread's width, as it is written, 'Will you not fear Me?' says God. 'Will you not tremble before Me, Who placed the sand

as a boundary of the sea, Who made an eternal law that
it can go no further?'" (Jeremiah 5.22) (Talmud, *Bava Batra* 73a)

Questions

1. What does this story teach us? How can wondrous
    occurrences in nature lead a person to become more
    reverent toward God?

2. The book of Leviticus commands us to fear our mother and
    father. What does fearing a parent mean to you? Is there a
    connection between fearing a parent and fearing God?

3. How can reciting blessings over such natural occurrences as
    a rainbow or a shooting star help to cultivate reverence for
    God?

4. Research the blessing that is recited every Shabbat prior to
    a new Jewish month. List the references to fear of God. Why
    do you think the rabbis chose to include them in the new
    month blessing?

5. The *Zohar* ii, 216a, says, "One who truly possesses the fear
    of God deserves to attain the love of God." What is the
    connection between the love and fear of God?

24. attentiveness— shemiat ha'ozen

Incline your ears and go to Me; listen
and your souls will live (Isaiah, 55.3).

The Hebrew term for attentiveness, *shemiat ha'ozen*, literally means a listening of the ear. Careful listening involves hearing, heeding, evaluating, understanding and obeying. *Pirke Avot*, 6.6, lists attentiveness as one of forty-eight virtues through which a person acquires knowledge of Torah.

Research studies have shown that communication is faulty. As a matter of fact, 90 percent of what a person hears goes in one ear and out the other. That is why it is virtuous to be a good listener. Being understanding, open-minded and patient are three keys to mastering the *middah* of attentiveness.

From Our Tradition

those to whom we should listen

This midrashic tale teaches us about the people to whom we must listen.

Rabbi Judah ben Shalom said, "If a poor person comes and pleads before another, that other does not listen to the poor one. If someone who is rich comes, the person receives and listens to the rich person immediately. God does not act in this way. All are equal before God—women, slaves, rich and poor" (*Exodus Rabbah* 21.4).

Questions

1. What is the essential difference between the human listener and God in the midrash above? Do you find that you are biased in your listening? In what circumstances do you listen with the greatest care?

2. The *Book of Proverbs* 12.15, says that "The one who listens to counsel is wise." How can listening to counsel make you a wise person?

3. One of the most important and well-known prayers is the Shema, which begins, "Listen O Israel, Adonai is Our God, Adonai is One" (*Deuteronomy* 6. 4). What does it mean to listen to God? By listening to God, have you ever heard God speak to you?

4. The Talmud (*Rosh ha-Shanah*, 25b) advises, "Happy are people whose great leaders listen to the small ones." What is the purpose of such advice? How could such advice apply to one's own family?

god's voice

This midrashic tale attempts to explain how people of various ages can come to hear God's voice.

God's voice went forth to the people of Israel according to their powers of obedience. The elders heard the voice according to their capacity. The adolescents, the youths, the children, the babies heard God's voice according to their capacity.

The women heard according to their capacity, and Moses too heard according to his capacity. For it is written, "As Moses spoke, God would answer him with the voice" (*Exodus*, 19.19). That is, God would answer Moses with a voice that Moses was able to hear (*Tanḥuma, Shemot* 25, 90b).

Questions

1. What is the meaning of hearing according to one's capacity? What are the implications of this story for a teacher?

2. There is a prayer that we recite on the High Holy Days called *Shema Koleinu*, Hear Our Voice. How do you know when God hears your voice? How can we hear God's voice?

3. When Moses took the record of the covenant and read it aloud to the people, the people said, "All that God has spoken we will do and we will hear" (Exodus 24.7). Why does the phrase "and we will hear" follow the phrase "and we will do"? What does hearing mean in the context of this biblical verse?

25. trustworthiness— emunah

The essence of trust is a tranquility of soul enjoyed by the one who trusts (Ibn Pakuda, Ḥovot ha-Levavot).

Anyone who has ever thought seriously about religion knows that *emunah,* trustworthiness or faith, is its foundation. The sages of the Talmud stress trustworthiness as a highly meritorious virtue, and they find fault with people of little faith.

The sages say that whoever deals with other people in a trusting way, with faithfulness, merits a seat next to God in the Divine court. *Emunah* begins when a person relies on God. A person who trusts in God has the ability to overcome all fears and personal anxieties.

Trustworthiness begins with learning to trust others. And with trust, says Ibn Pakuda, comes a tranquility of the soul.

From Our Tradition
the sacrifice of isaac

Following is an excerpt from the biblical story of Abraham and his son Isaac. The story clearly demonstrates the trust that Isaac had for his father Abraham and the trust that Abraham must have had for God in this seemingly irrational mission.

And Isaac spoke to Abraham his father and said, "My father."

And Abraham said, "Here am I, my son."

And Isaac said, "Behold the fire and the wood, but where is the lamb for a burnt offering?"

And Abraham said, "God will provide Himself the lamb for a burnt offering, my son."

So they went both of them together. And they came to the place that God had told him. And Abraham built the altar there, and laid the wood in order, and bound Isaac his son, and laid him on the altar upon the wood. And Abraham stretched forth his hand and took the knife to slay his son. And the angel of God called to him out of heaven, and said, "Abraham, Abraham."

And he said, "'Here I am."

And the angel said, "Do not lay your hand upon the lad, neither do you anything to him, for now I know that you are a God-fearing man, seeing that you have not with-held your son, your only son, from Me" (Genesis 22. 7-12).

Questions

1. If you were Abraham and were told by God to sacrifice your son, do you think you would attempt to carry out the mission without challenging it? Are there any times when one ought not to trust another?

2. If someone you trust asks you to do something of which you are somewhat suspicious, should you challenge that person by asking questions, or should you simply put your full trust in that person?

3. Rabbi Isaac Kook, former Chief Rabbi of Israel, once said that "Faith is the song of life." What do you think he meant by this statement?

3. Jeremiah says, "Blessed is the person who trusts God" (Jeremiah 17.2). In what way is a person who trusts in God blessed?

4. Who are the people you most trust? What are the attributes and virtues of a trustworthy person?

ticket to heaven

The following Hasidic tale shows the concern for trust and faith in interpersonal relations.

> There was a man who never studied Torah except on Shabbat, because on all the weekdays he conducted business. He asked a sage, "What virtue will outweigh all the time I have spent in business matters and bring me eternal life in the world to come?"
>
> The sage answered him, "You who engage in business must act toward all others with trust" (*Otzar Sefer Hasidim, Emunah*).

Questions

1. What is the moral of this Hasidic story? What can an employer do to gain the trust of his employees? What can employees do to raise the level of trust put in them by their employer?

2. What are the pitfalls of having "blind faith" in someone?

3. Do you think it is possible to survive life's hardships without some kind of faith? Other than God, in what or

whom might a person have faith? Why might it seem more acceptable to have faith in things other than God?

4. *Sefer Ḥasidim* says, "When you make a friend, begin by testing him, and be in no hurry to trust him." What do you think about this advice? Why should one be careful about trusting another person?

looking back and looking ahead

Despite the many texts that insist on the primacy of ethics and good behavior, many Jewish people still tend to associate being religious solely with observing customs and rituals. If someone asks, "Is so-and-so religious?" the response invariably is based on the person's level of ritual observance. "She keeps kosher and observes Shabbat and festivals, and therefore she is religious."

It is true that observing customs and rituals is part of keeping Judaism, but it is equally true that Judaism is very concerned with decency and goodness. Ethical behavior is one of God's central demands. Good people always strive to do better for themselves and other people, working toward the ultimate goal of the perfection of the world.

I hope that you will make Torah study a regular part of your life. Always remember that by studying Torah and acting on what you learn you will be constantly reminded of the virtues necessary to become a better person. Love justice and decency and continue to thirst for righteousness, for that is the essence of living life as a human being.

Centuries ago Rabbi Levi said, "Whoever thinks to himself before going to sleep, 'When I wake the next day, I will do good things for so-and-so,' that person will share great joy with the good people in the future, in the future world, as it is written, 'There is joy for people who make plans to do good'" (Midrash, *Psalms* 12.1).

glossary of sources

Following is a listing of the sources quoted.

Avot de Rabbi Natan. Small Talmudic tractate that expands upon *Ethics of the Fathers*. It was written by Rabbi Nathan the Babylonian.

Babylonian Talmud. The first sourcebook for Jewish law. It is composed of the Mishnah, a six-volume collection edited by Judah the Prince around 200 C.E., and the Gemara, which explains the Mishnah and was compiled in approximately 500 C.E.

Code of Jewish Law. Authoritative law code written by Joseph Karo, a legal codifier of the sixteenth century.

Jerusalem Talmud. Compilation of laws and discussion of the teachers in Israel, mainly in the academy of Tiberias in the Galilee region. Much shorter than the Babylonian Talmud and less authoritative.

Menorat ha-Maor. Midrashic book written by Isaac Abohav, a fourteenth-century sage. It emphasizes Jewish ethics.

Midrash. Refers to non-legal sections of the Talmud and the rabbinic books that contain biblical interpretations in the spirit of legend.

Midrash Rabbah. Collection of midrashim concerning the Five Books of Moses and the Five Megillot.

Midrash Tanḥuma. Attributed to Rabbi Tanḥuma bar Abba, this work consists of discourses about the opening verse of the Torah portion designated for each week.

Mishnah Torah. First comprehensive codification of Jewish law, by Moses Maimonides. (Twelfth century C.E.)

Orhot Tzaddikim. *The Ways of the Righteous*, a book of virtues that has spawned some eighty editions since the sixteenth century.

Pirke Avot. Talmudic tractate containing pithy sayings and ethical teachings of the rabbinic sages from the third century B.C.E. to the third century C.E.

Pirke de Rabbi Eliezer. Tannaitic midrash on the *Book of Genesis*. "Tanaaim" refers to the teachers living during the first two centuries of the common era.

Sefer Ha–Musar. Ethical treatise written by the sixteenth-century Algerian sage Rabbi Yehuda ibn Kalaaz.

Sefer Hasidim. Homiletical text written by Judah the Hassid, thirteenth century C.E.

Sefer Maalot ha–Middot. An anthology of Jewish virtues written by the thirteenth-century sage Yehiel ben Yekutiel ben Binyman Harofe.

Yalkut Shimoni. Midrashic collection relating to all of the books of the Bible, compiled by Shimon Kayyara ha-Darshan in the thirteenth century C.E.